101 Brilliant Prompts to Boost Your Earnings

Using AI to Achieve Business Success and Make a Million Dollars

1. Chapter

Leveraging AI for Market Research

In this book, I aim to delve deep into the world of AI and its revolutionary impact on market research. With three key chapters - Understanding Consumer Behavior with AI, Analyzing Market Trends through AI, and Identifying Profitable Niches with AI - I will explore the cutting-edge technologies and strategies that are reshaping the way we understand and interact with consumers.

The first chapter, Understanding Consumer Behavior with AI, will highlight the power of AI in unlocking valuable insights into consumer preferences, motivations, and behaviors. By harnessing the capabilities of machine learning algorithms and predictive analytics, businesses can gain a deeper understanding of their target audience and tailor their marketing strategies accordingly.

In the second chapter, Analyzing Market Trends through AI, I will showcase how AI is revolutionizing the way we identify and capitalize on emerging trends in the market. From sentiment analysis and social media monitoring to real-time data analytics, AI enables businesses to stay ahead of the curve and adapt to changing market dynamics with agility and precision.

Finally, in the third chapter, Identifying Profitable Niches with AI, I will demonstrate how AI can help businesses uncover untapped opportunities and niches within their market. By leveraging advanced algorithms and data mining techniques, businesses can pinpoint high-potential segments and develop targeted strategies to maximize profitability and growth.

Join me on this exciting journey into the world of AI and market research, where innovation knows no bounds and insights abound. Let's harness the power of artificial intelligence to drive business success and unlock new possibilities in the ever-evolving landscape of consumer behavior and market trends. Welcome to the future of market research - welcome to the world of AI.

- Subchapter 1:
Understanding Consumer
Behavior with AI

Introduction to AI and Consumer
Behavior
In today's fast-paced digital
world, understanding consumer
behavior is more important than
ever. With the rise of artificial
intelligence (AI), businesses have
a powerful tool at their disposal
to analyze and predict consumer
preferences and trends. In this
chapter, we will explore how AI
is revolutionizing the way

companies understand and engage with their customers.

1.1 What is AI?

Artificial intelligence refers to the ability of machines to learn from data, make decisions, and perform tasks that typically require human intelligence. AI technologies such as machine learning, natural language processing, and computer vision are enabling businesses to analyze vast amounts of data and extract meaningful insights.

1.2 How AI is transforming consumer behavior analysis

Traditionally, consumer behavior analysis relied on surveys, focus groups, and market research to understand customer preferences. However, with the advent of AI, companies can now tap into a wealth of online data to gain deeper insights into consumer behavior.

AI-powered algorithms can analyze social media posts, online reviews, and search data to uncover patterns and trends in consumer behavior. By leveraging machine learning models, businesses can predict customer preferences, identify potential influencers, and personalize marketing campaigns to target specific audience segments.

1.3 The benefits of using AI in

consumer behavior analysis
There are several key benefits to using AI in consumer behavior analysis. Firstly, AI algorithms can process large volumes of data quickly and accurately, enabling companies to make informed decisions in real-time. Secondly, AI can identify subtle patterns and correlations in consumer behavior that may not be apparent to human analysts. By leveraging AI, businesses can gain a competitive edge by understanding consumer preferences and tailoring their products and services to meet evolving customer needs. In addition, AI can help companies

identify market trends and opportunities for growth, allowing them to stay ahead of the competition.

1.4 Challenges in using AI for consumer behavior analysis

While AI offers many benefits for consumer behavior analysis, there are also challenges that companies must overcome. One of the main challenges is ensuring the accuracy and reliability of AI algorithms. Biases in the data or model can lead to inaccurate predictions and flawed insights.

Another challenge is the ethical considerations of using AI to analyze consumer behavior.

Companies must ensure that they are transparent about how they use customer data and protect consumer privacy. By addressing these challenges, businesses can harness the power of AI to gain a deeper understanding of consumer behavior and drive business growth.

1.5 Conclusion

In conclusion, AI is transforming the way companies understand and analyze consumer behavior. By leveraging AI-powered algorithms and machine learning models, businesses can gain valuable insights into customer preferences, trends, and behaviors. As AI continues to evolve, companies that embrace these technologies will be better positioned to succeed in today's competitive marketplace.

- Subchapter 2:

Analyzing Market Trends through AI

The Rise of AI in Market Analysis

In recent years, artificial intelligence has revolutionized the way businesses analyze market trends. By harnessing the power of AI algorithms, companies can now gather, process, and interpret vast amounts of data to gain valuable insights into consumer behavior and industry developments. In this chapter, we will explore how AI is transforming market analysis and shaping the future of business strategy.

The Role of AI in Market Analysis

Traditional market analysis methods often rely on manual data collection and analysis, which can be time-consuming and prone to human error. With the advent of AI technology, companies can now automate these processes and leverage machine learning algorithms to extract meaningful patterns and trends from large datasets. By using AI-powered tools such as predictive analytics and natural language processing, businesses can quickly identify market opportunities, forecast trends, and make informed decisions based on data-driven insights.

One of the key advantages of AI in market analysis is its ability to process and analyze unstructured data sources, such as social media posts, online reviews, and multimedia content.

By analyzing these diverse datasets, AI algorithms can uncover valuable information about consumer preferences, sentiment, and behavior, helping companies better understand their target audience and tailor their marketing strategies accordingly.

AI-powered market analysis tools also enable businesses to track competitor activities, monitor industry trends, and identify emerging market opportunities. By continuously analyzing market data in real-time, companies can stay ahead of the competition and adapt their strategies to changing market conditions. Furthermore, AI algorithms can help businesses optimize pricing strategies, forecast demand, and personalize marketing campaigns to maximize customer engagement and drive sales.

Challenges and Future Trends

While AI offers numerous benefits for market analysis, there are also challenges and limitations that businesses need to consider. One of the main challenges is the quality and reliability of data used for analysis. Inaccurate or biased data can lead to flawed insights and incorrect decision-making, highlighting the importance of data quality and integrity in AI-driven market analysis.

Another challenge is the need for skilled personnel to develop and deploy AI algorithms for market analysis. As AI technology continues to evolve rapidly, businesses must invest in training and upskilling their workforce to harness the full potential of AI tools and ensure accurate and reliable results.

Looking ahead, the future of AI in market analysis holds immense potential for innovation and growth. Advancements in AI technology, such as deep learning and cognitive computing, promise to further enhance the capabilities of market analysis tools and provide businesses with even more sophisticated insights and predictions. Additionally, the integration of AI with other emerging technologies, such as blockchain and IoT, will open up new possibilities for data collection, analysis, and decision-making in the market.

In conclusion, AI is revolutionizing market analysis by enabling businesses to leverage advanced algorithms and data-driven insights to gain a competitive edge in today's fast-paced business environment. By embracing AI technology and investing in skilled professionals, companies can unlock new opportunities, drive growth, and stay ahead of the curve in an increasingly digital and data-driven market landscape.

Identifying Profitable Niches with AI

Identifying Profitable Niches with AI
In today's fast-paced and dynamic business environment, staying ahead of the competition requires more than just a good idea. Success in the marketplace is driven by identifying profitable niches and capitalizing on them before your competitors do. This is where artificial intelligence (AI) comes in.

AI has revolutionized the way businesses operate, providing unprecedented insights into consumer behavior and market trends. By leveraging AI technology, companies can gain a competitive edge by identifying profitable niches that others may overlook.
One of the key benefits of using AI for niche identification is its ability to process vast amounts of data quickly and accurately. By analyzing consumer behavior, market trends, and competitor strategies, AI can identify emerging niches that present lucrative opportunities for growth.

For example, a company selling health and wellness products may use AI to analyze social media trends and online search data to identify a growing interest in organic skincare products. By leveraging this insight, the company can develop and market a new line of organic skincare products to capitalize on this emerging niche. AI can also help businesses optimize their marketing strategies by identifying the most effective channels for reaching target customers within a specific niche. By analyzing user engagement data and customer feedback, AI can tailor

marketing campaigns to
resonate with the preferences
and interests of niche audiences.
Furthermore, AI can assist
businesses in monitoring and
adapting to changes in the
market landscape in real-time.
By continuously analyzing
market data and consumer
behavior, AI can alert businesses
to shifts in demand or emerging
competitive threats, enabling
proactive decision-making to
stay ahead of the curve.
In conclusion, leveraging AI for
niche identification is essential
for businesses looking to thrive
in today's competitive
marketplace. By harnessing the

power of AI to analyze data, gain insights, and make informed decisions, companies can identify profitable niches and capitalize on emerging opportunities for growth and success. The key to success in the digital age lies in embracing AI technology and using it to drive innovation and competitive advantage.

2. Chapter

Enhancing Customer Engagement with AI

In this chapter, we will delve into the fascinating world of Artificial Intelligence and its applications in enhancing customer engagement. As technology continues to advance at a rapid pace, businesses are finding new ways to leverage AI to personalize customer experiences, improve customer service, and optimize targeted marketing campaigns.

The first section of this chapter will focus on how AI is revolutionizing the way businesses interact with their customers by personalizing their experiences. Through advanced data analytics and machine learning algorithms, companies can now tailor their products and services to meet the unique needs and preferences of individual customers. This not only enhances customer satisfaction and loyalty but also drives revenue growth and competitive advantage.

Next, we will explore the role of AI chatbots in improving customer service. AI-powered chatbots are becoming increasingly popular as a cost-effective solution for handling customer inquiries, resolving issues, and providing real-time support. By automating repetitive tasks and delivering instant responses, businesses can streamline their operations, increase efficiency, and deliver a seamless customer experience. Lastly, we will discuss how businesses can utilize AI for targeted marketing campaigns. By analyzing vast amounts of customer data, AI can help companies identify trends, predict consumer behavior, and create personalized marketing strategies that resonate with their target audience. This enables businesses to reach the right customers with the right message at the right time, maximizing ROI and driving business growth.

Overall, this chapter will provide valuable insights into how AI is transforming customer engagement and empowering businesses to deliver exceptional experiences to their customers. From personalizing customer experiences to improving customer service and optimizing marketing campaigns, AI is revolutionizing the way businesses interact with their customers and driving success in the digital age.

- Subchapter 1:

Personalizing Customer Experiences through AI

Personalizing Customer
Experiences through AI
In today's digital age, businesses
are constantly looking for ways
to improve customer
experiences and increase
customer satisfaction. One of
the most effective ways to
achieve this is through the use of
artificial intelligence (AI). AI has
the ability to personalize

customer experiences in a way that was never before possible, allowing businesses to cater to the individual needs and preferences of each customer. One of the key ways in which AI can personalize customer experiences is through the use of recommendation engines. These engines analyze customer data, such as past purchases and browsing history, to provide personalized recommendations for products or services that the customer is likely to be interested in. This not only helps customers discover new products that they may not have otherwise come across, but also increases the likelihood of a purchase being made.

Another way in which AI can personalize customer experiences is through the use of chatbots. Chatbots are AI-powered virtual assistants that can interact with customers in real-time, providing them with personalized recommendations, answering their questions, and assisting them with their purchases. By using chatbots, businesses can provide customers with a personalized and efficient service, leading to increased customer satisfaction and loyalty.

AI can also be used to

personalize marketing campaigns, allowing businesses to target customers with relevant and timely messages. By analyzing customer data, AI can determine the best time and channel to reach each customer, increasing the likelihood of a successful marketing campaign. This level of personalization not only improves customer engagement, but also leads to higher conversion rates and increased revenue for businesses. Overall, AI offers businesses the opportunity to personalize customer experiences in a way that was previously unimaginable. By harnessing the power of AI, businesses can better understand their customers, anticipate their needs, and provide them with personalized and engaging experiences. As AI continues to advance, the possibilities for personalizing customer experiences are endless, making it an essential tool for businesses looking to thrive in the digital age.

Improving Customer Service with AI Chatbots

The Rise of AI Chatbots in Customer Service
In today's fast-paced world, customer service has become more important than ever. With the rise of e-commerce and online businesses, consumers expect quick and efficient responses to their queries and concerns. This has led to the increasing use of AI chatbots in

customer service.

AI chatbots are virtual assistants that use artificial intelligence to interact with customers in a natural language conversation. These chatbots can answer questions, provide information, and even assist with transactions. They never get tired, are available 24/7, and can handle multiple customer inquiries simultaneously.

The use of AI chatbots in customer service has proven to be highly effective in improving customer satisfaction and loyalty. Customers appreciate the instant responses and personalized interactions that chatbots provide. Businesses benefit from the cost savings and efficiency gains that come with automating customer service processes.

One of the key advantages of using AI chatbots in customer service is their ability to learn and adapt over time. Through machine learning algorithms, chatbots can analyze customer interactions, identify patterns, and improve their responses accordingly. This means that the more a chatbot interacts with customers, the better it becomes at understanding their needs and preferences.

Another benefit of AI chatbots is

their scalability. Unlike human agents, chatbots can handle an unlimited number of customer inquiries simultaneously. This makes them ideal for businesses that experience high volumes of customer interactions or sudden spikes in traffic. Chatbots can also be easily customized to suit the needs of different industries and specific business requirements.

Overall, AI chatbots have revolutionized the way businesses approach customer service. By leveraging the power of artificial intelligence, businesses can provide faster, more efficient, and more personalized customer support. In the following chapters, we will explore the various ways in which AI chatbots can be used to improve customer service across different industries.

- Subchapter 3:

Utilizing AI for Targeted Marketing Campaigns

Utilizing AI for Targeted Marketing Campaigns

In today's digital age, businesses are constantly looking for new ways to reach their target audience with personalized and targeted marketing campaigns. With the rise of artificial intelligence (AI), companies now have the ability to leverage this technology to create more effective and efficient marketing strategies.

One of the key benefits of using AI for targeted marketing campaigns is the ability to analyze large amounts of data in real-time. AI algorithms can sift through vast amounts of customer data, including demographics, purchasing behavior, and online interactions, to identify patterns and trends that would be impossible for humans to detect.

By understanding these patterns, businesses can create highly targeted marketing campaigns that resonate with their audience on a deeper level. For example, AI can be used to segment customers into specific groups based on their preferences and behaviors, allowing companies to tailor their messages and offers accordingly.

Another advantage of using AI

for targeted marketing campaigns is the ability to automate the process of campaign optimization. AI-powered tools can continuously monitor the performance of marketing campaigns, adjusting targeting parameters, messaging, and delivery channels in real-time to maximize results. Furthermore, AI can also help businesses personalize their marketing content at scale. By analyzing individual customer data, AI algorithms can generate personalized recommendations, product suggestions, and offers that are more likely to resonate with each customer, ultimately increasing conversions and driving sales.

In addition to improving the efficiency and effectiveness of marketing campaigns, AI can also help businesses better understand their customers. By analyzing data from various touchpoints, such as social media, email, and website interactions, AI can provide valuable insights into customer preferences, behaviors, and sentiment.

Overall, the use of AI for targeted marketing campaigns represents a significant opportunity for businesses to improve their marketing efforts and drive better results. By leveraging the power of AI to analyze data, automate processes, and personalize content, companies can create more engaging and relevant campaigns that connect with customers on a deeper level. As we continue to see advancements in AI technology, the possibilities for using AI in marketing will only continue to grow. By staying ahead of the curve and embracing this technology, businesses can position themselves for success in an increasingly competitive digital landscape.

Chapter 3:

Optimizing Business Operations with AI

In today's rapidly evolving digital landscape, businesses are constantly seeking ways to streamline their operations, improve efficiency, and stay ahead of the competition. One of the most transformative

technologies that has emerged
in recent years is artificial
intelligence (AI). With its ability
to analyze vast amounts of data,
identify patterns, and make
intelligent decisions, AI has the
potential to revolutionize the
way companies operate.
In this book, we will delve into
the world of AI and explore how
it can be leveraged to optimize
business operations. From
automating routine tasks to
enhancing supply chain
management and improving
decision-making through
analytics, AI offers a plethora of
opportunities for organizations
to gain a competitive edge.

The first subchapter focuses on automating routine tasks with AI. By delegating mundane, repetitive tasks to AI-powered systems, businesses can free up valuable time and resources, allowing employees to focus on more strategic initiatives. We will discuss the benefits of task automation, the different technologies involved, and how organizations can effectively implement AI into their day-to-day operations.

Next, we will explore how AI can enhance supply chain management. From predictive analytics to real-time monitoring, AI offers a range of tools that can help businesses optimize their supply chains, reduce costs, and improve overall efficiency. We will delve into case studies and best practices to showcase how leading companies are using AI to revolutionize their supply chain processes.

Finally, we will turn our attention to how AI can improve decision-making through advanced analytics. By leveraging AI-powered algorithms, businesses can gain valuable insights from their data, enabling them to make informed decisions that drive growth and profitability. We will discuss the various analytical techniques available, as well as real-world examples of organizations that have successfully integrated AI analytics into their decision-making processes.

In conclusion, this book aims to provide readers with a comprehensive understanding of how AI can be used to optimize various aspects of business operations. Whether you are a small startup or a large enterprise, embracing AI technologies can unlock new opportunities and propel your organization towards success in the digital age. So, join me on this journey as we explore the transformative power of AI in optimizing business operations.

- Subchapter 1:

Automating Routine Tasks with AI

The Rise of Artificial Intelligence In the fast-paced world we live in today, time is a precious commodity. From the moment we wake up in the morning to the moment we go to bed at night, we are constantly bombarded with tasks that need to be completed. Whether it's responding to emails, scheduling meetings, or keeping track of deadlines, our days are filled with routine tasks that can eat away at our productivity.

But what if there was a way to automate these mundane tasks and free up valuable time for more important work? Enter artificial intelligence, or AI for short. AI has been making waves in recent years as a powerful tool for streamlining processes and increasing efficiency. By harnessing the power of AI, businesses and individuals alike can automate routine tasks and

focus on what truly matters.
One of the key benefits of AI is
its ability to learn from data and
adapt to changing circumstances.
This means that AI can
continuously improve its
performance over time, making
it an invaluable asset for any
organization. By analyzing
patterns and trends in data, AI
can make predictions and
recommendations that help us
make better decisions.
Take for example the task of
scheduling meetings. This is
something that most of us dread,
as it can be time-consuming and
frustrating. But with AI,
scheduling meetings becomes a

breeze. AI-powered tools can analyze your calendar, preferences, and availability to suggest the best times for a meeting. Not only does this save time, but it also ensures that meetings are scheduled at optimal times for all parties involved.

Another common task that can be automated with AI is email management. We all know how overwhelming our inboxes can be, with hundreds of emails flooding in each day. AI can help by intelligently sorting and prioritizing emails, ensuring that you never miss an important message. By learning your preferences and habits, AI can even draft responses to emails on your behalf, saving you even more time.

But the potential of AI goes far beyond just automating routine tasks. With advancements in machine learning and natural language processing, AI is now being used to solve complex problems across a wide range of industries. From healthcare to finance to transportation, AI is revolutionizing the way we work and live.

In the field of healthcare, for example, AI is being used to analyze medical images and identify patterns that human doctors might miss. This can lead to earlier detection of diseases and more accurate diagnoses, ultimately saving lives. In finance, AI is being used to detect fraudulent activity and predict market trends, helping businesses make smarter financial decisions.

As we continue to push the boundaries of what AI can do, the possibilities are endless. From self-driving cars to virtual assistants, AI is reshaping the world around us in ways we never thought possible. And as we embrace this technology and harness its power, we can unlock new levels of productivity and innovation.

So the next time you find yourself drowning in routine tasks, remember that AI is here to help. By automating the mundane and repetitive tasks that bog us down, we can reclaim our time and focus on what truly matters. With AI by our side, the possibilities are limitless.

Enhancing Supply Chain Management with AI

The Rise of AI in Supply Chain Management
In a world where technology is constantly evolving, artificial intelligence (AI) has emerged as a game-changer in the field of supply chain management. With its ability to analyze vast amounts of data and make real-time decisions, AI is transforming how companies operate and

manage their supply chains.
The traditional approach to
supply chain management
involved manual processes that
were time-consuming and prone
to errors. But with the advent of
AI, companies now have access
to advanced algorithms and
machine learning techniques
that can optimize every aspect of
their supply chain.
One of the key advantages of AI
in supply chain management is
its ability to predict demand and
optimize inventory levels. By
analyzing historical data and
external factors such as market
trends and weather patterns, AI
can help companies forecast

demand more accurately and ensure that they have the right amount of inventory on hand at all times.

AI can also improve the efficiency of logistics operations by optimizing routes, reducing transportation costs, and minimizing delays. By analyzing real-time data from sensors and IoT devices, AI can identify potential bottlenecks in the supply chain and suggest alternative routes or transportation modes to ensure on-time delivery.

Furthermore, AI can enhance the visibility and transparency of supply chain operations by providing real-time tracking of goods and inventory. This not only helps companies meet customer expectations for fast and reliable delivery but also allows them to quickly respond to any disruptions or delays in the supply chain.

Overall, the integration of AI in supply chain management has the potential to revolutionize the way companies plan, execute, and optimize their supply chain operations. By leveraging the power of AI, companies can achieve greater efficiency, reduce costs, and improve customer satisfaction.

In the following chapters, we will

explore in detail how AI is reshaping the supply chain landscape and the various ways in which companies can harness this technology to drive business growth and success. Stay tuned for more insights and practical tips on how to leverage AI in supply chain management.

Improving Decision-Making with AI Analytics

The Rise of AI Analytics in Decision-Making
In the fast-paced world of modern business, making informed decisions is crucial for success. With the exponential growth of data and the increasing complexity of markets, traditional decision-making processes are no longer sufficient. This is where AI

analytics comes in.

Artificial Intelligence (AI) has revolutionized the way organizations analyze data and make decisions. By leveraging advanced algorithms and machine learning techniques, AI analytics can uncover hidden patterns and insights from vast amounts of data that human analysts simply cannot process on their own.

One of the key advantages of AI analytics is its ability to automate and streamline decision-making processes. By using AI-powered tools and technologies, businesses can quickly and accurately analyze data, identify trends, and make predictions with a high level of accuracy. This not only saves time and resources but also reduces the risk of human error. Furthermore, AI analytics can provide organizations with a competitive edge by enabling them to make data-driven decisions in real-time. By continuously monitoring and analyzing data, businesses can quickly adapt to changing market conditions and seize new opportunities as they arise. Another major benefit of AI analytics is its ability to improve decision-making by providing valuable insights and recommendations. By analyzing historical data and identifying patterns, AI can help organizations predict future outcomes and optimize their strategies accordingly.

For example, in the field of finance, AI analytics can be used to predict stock prices, detect fraudulent transactions, and optimize investment portfolios.

In healthcare, AI can analyze medical records and genetic data to diagnose diseases, recommend treatments, and improve patient outcomes.

Overall, AI analytics has the potential to transform decision-making across industries and drive innovation and growth. By harnessing the power of AI, organizations can gain a deeper understanding of their data, make more accurate predictions, and ultimately make better decisions.

In the following chapters of this book, we will explore the various applications of AI analytics in decision-making and provide practical examples of how businesses can leverage these technologies to drive success. So buckle up and get ready to embark on a journey into the exciting world of AI analytics. The future of decision-making is here, and it's powered by AI.

Chapter 4:

Increasing Sales Conversions through AI

In today's rapidly evolving digital landscape, harnessing the power of Artificial Intelligence (AI) has become crucial for businesses looking to stay ahead of the competition. AI has revolutionized the way companies approach sales and marketing, offering unprecedented insights into

customer behavior and preferences that were previously impossible to obtain. In this book, we will explore the impact of AI on increasing sales conversions, focusing on three key subchapters that delve into different aspects of AI integration in sales strategies.
Subchapter 1: Predicting Customer Buying Patterns with AI
One of the most significant advantages of AI in sales is its ability to predict customer buying patterns with remarkable accuracy. By analyzing vast amounts of data, AI algorithms can identify trends and patterns

in customer behavior, allowing businesses to tailor their marketing strategies to target specific audiences more effectively. In this subchapter, we will discuss the various ways in which AI can be used to predict customer buying patterns and optimize sales strategies accordingly.

Subchapter 2: Implementing AI-Powered Sales Funnel Optimization

The sales funnel is a critical component of any sales strategy, representing the journey that customers take from initial awareness to final purchase. AI can play a crucial role in

optimizing the sales funnel by automating repetitive tasks, personalizing the customer experience, and identifying opportunities for upselling and cross-selling. We will explore how businesses can leverage AI to streamline the sales funnel and drive higher conversion rates in this subchapter.
Subchapter 3: Leveraging AI for Upselling and Cross-Selling Strategies
Upselling and cross-selling are proven strategies for maximizing revenue from existing customers, but identifying the right opportunities can be challenging without the right insights. AI can

analyze customer data to identify potential upsell and cross-sell opportunities, enabling businesses to offer relevant products or services at the right time. In this subchapter, we will discuss how AI can be leveraged to implement effective upselling and cross-selling strategies that drive revenue growth and enhance customer loyalty.

By delving into these three key subchapters, this book aims to provide readers with a comprehensive understanding of how AI can be used to increase sales conversions and drive business growth. Whether you are a seasoned sales professional or just beginning to explore the possibilities of AI in sales, this book will equip you with the knowledge and insights needed to harness the full potential of AI in your sales strategies.

- Subchapter 1:

Predicting Customer Buying Patterns with AI

The Power of AI in Predicting Customer Buying Patterns
As a seasoned copywriter and author of best sellers, I have

witnessed firsthand the transformative power of artificial intelligence (AI) in various industries. One area where AI has truly revolutionized the way businesses operate is in predicting customer buying patterns.

Gone are the days of relying solely on traditional market research and gut instincts to understand consumer behavior. With the vast amounts of data available today, businesses can leverage AI algorithms to analyze this data and accurately predict what customers will buy next. But how exactly does AI do this? Let's delve into the intricacies of how AI is able to predict customer buying patterns with precision and accuracy.

First and foremost, AI relies on machine learning algorithms to sift through vast amounts of data and identify patterns and trends. By analyzing historical purchasing data, AI can identify correlations between different variables, such as demographics, purchase history, and even external factors like weather and economic conditions.

These algorithms then use this data to create predictive models that can forecast future buying patterns. For example, a retailer may use AI to analyze past purchasing behavior and predict which products a customer is likely to buy based on their browsing history, previous purchases, and even their social media activity.

But AI doesn't stop at just predicting what customers will buy next. It can also personalize recommendations and promotions based on individual preferences and behaviors. By leveraging AI-powered recommendation engines, businesses can deliver targeted offers and product suggestions that are tailored to each customer's unique tastes and preferences.

Furthermore, AI can help businesses optimize their marketing strategies by identifying the most effective channels and messages to reach customers. By analyzing customer interactions and responses to marketing campaigns, AI can provide insights into what resonates with customers and what doesn't, allowing businesses to refine their approach for maximum impact.

In essence, AI enables businesses to move beyond reactive marketing tactics and adopt a proactive approach to understanding and engaging

with customers. By leveraging the power of AI to predict customer buying patterns, businesses can stay ahead of the curve and deliver personalized experiences that drive loyalty and revenue.
But with great power comes great responsibility. As AI continues to evolve and become more sophisticated, businesses must prioritize ethical considerations and data privacy to ensure that customer trust is maintained. Transparency and accountability are key to building and maintaining strong relationships with customers in the age of AI.

In conclusion, the ability to predict customer buying patterns with AI is a game-changer for businesses looking to stay competitive in today's fast-paced marketplace. By harnessing the predictive power of AI, businesses can unlock new opportunities for growth, enhance customer experiences, and drive long-term success. The future of marketing belongs to those who embrace AI and leverage its capabilities to anticipate and meet the evolving needs of customers.

Implementing AI-Powered Sales Funnel Optimization

The Rise of AI in Sales Funnel Optimization

In the ever-evolving world of sales and marketing, staying ahead of the curve is essential for success. With the rapid advancement of artificial intelligence (AI) technology, businesses are now able to harness the power of data and automation to optimize their

sales funnels like never before.
In this chapter, we will explore
the rise of AI in sales funnel
optimization and how it can
revolutionize the way businesses
drive revenue.

The traditional sales funnel
model has long been the
cornerstone of sales and
marketing strategies, guiding
prospects from awareness to
conversion. However, with the
emergence of AI technology,
businesses now have the ability
to analyze vast amounts of data
in real-time, allowing for more
personalized and targeted
marketing efforts.

One of the key benefits of

implementing AI-powered sales funnel optimization is the ability to predict customer behavior and tailor marketing strategies accordingly. By analyzing past customer interactions and purchasing patterns, AI algorithms can identify potential leads and guide them through the sales funnel with personalized content and recommendations.

Furthermore, AI can automate repetitive tasks such as lead scoring, email marketing, and customer segmentation, freeing up valuable time for sales and marketing teams to focus on strategic initiatives. This not only increases efficiency but also allows businesses to scale their operations and reach a larger audience.

Another major advantage of AI-powered sales funnel optimization is the ability to continuously improve and refine marketing strategies based on real-time data analysis. By tracking key performance indicators (KPIs) and monitoring customer engagement metrics, businesses can identify areas for improvement and make data-driven decisions to optimize their sales funnel for maximum results.

Overall, the rise of AI in sales

funnel optimization represents a major shift in the way businesses approach sales and marketing. By harnessing the power of data and automation, businesses can create more personalized and targeted marketing campaigns, increase efficiency, and drive revenue growth. In the following chapters, we will delve deeper into the practical applications of AI-powered sales funnel optimization and provide actionable insights for businesses looking to stay ahead of the competition.

Leveraging AI for Upselling and Cross-Selling Strategies

The Rise of Artificial Intelligence in Sales
In today's digital age, businesses are constantly seeking new ways to boost their sales and increase revenue. One of the most effective tools for achieving this is artificial intelligence (AI). AI has revolutionized the way companies approach sales,

allowing for more personalized and targeted outreach to customers. In this chapter, we will explore how AI is being leveraged for upselling and cross-selling strategies.

AI has the ability to analyze vast amounts of data in real time, allowing businesses to better understand customer behavior and preferences. By utilizing machine learning algorithms, AI can identify patterns and trends that may not be immediately obvious to human sales representatives. This information can then be used to tailor product recommendations to individual customers, increasing the likelihood of a successful upsell or cross-sell. Furthermore, AI can automate the upselling and cross-selling process, reducing the burden on sales teams and freeing up valuable time for other tasks. For example, AI-powered chatbots can engage with customers in real time, offering personalized product suggestions based on their browsing history and previous purchases. This level of personalized interaction can significantly increase conversion rates and drive revenue growth. Another key benefit of AI in sales is its ability to predict customer behavior and anticipate future

needs. By analyzing historical data and customer interactions, AI can identify when a customer may be ready for an upsell or cross-sell. This proactive approach allows businesses to capitalize on opportunities in real time, maximizing the potential for increased sales.
In conclusion, AI is revolutionizing the way businesses approach upselling and cross-selling strategies. By leveraging the power of artificial intelligence, companies can gain valuable insights into customer behavior, automate the sales process, and predict future needs. As AI continues to evolve,

the possibilities for driving revenue growth through upselling and cross-selling are endless. Stay tuned for the next chapter, where we will explore practical applications of AI in sales.

5. Chapter 5:

Harnessing AI for Financial Planning and Management

Introduction
Welcome to the world of Artificial Intelligence (AI) and its applications in financial planning and management. In this book, we will explore how AI algorithms can revolutionize the way we approach financial forecasting, budgeting, expense

tracking, and investment strategies.

In today's fast-paced and complex financial landscape, traditional methods of financial planning and management are no longer sufficient. The rapid advancements in AI technology have paved the way for new and innovative solutions that can help individuals and organizations make better-informed decisions, optimize resources, and achieve financial success.

In this book, we will delve into three key subchapters that highlight the power of AI in transforming the way we handle finances:

Subchapter 1: Using AI Algorithms for Financial Forecasting

AI algorithms have the ability to analyze vast amounts of data with speed and accuracy, enabling us to generate more precise financial forecasts. By leveraging machine learning and predictive analytics, we can uncover hidden patterns, trends, and insights that traditional forecasting methods may overlook. In this subchapter, we will explore how AI can enhance our forecasting capabilities and help us make more informed decisions about our financial future.

Subchapter 2: Automated Budgeting and Expense Tracking with AI

Budgeting and expense tracking are essential components of effective financial management. AI can automate these processes, taking into account various factors such as income, expenses, savings goals, and spending habits. With AI-driven tools, individuals and businesses can create personalized budgets, track expenses in real-time, and receive intelligent recommendations to optimize their financial health. In this subchapter, we will discuss the

benefits of using AI for
budgeting and expense tracking
and how it can empower us to
take control of our finances.

Subchapter 3: Minimizing Risks
and Maximizing Returns with AI
Investment Strategies

Investing is inherently risky, but
AI can help mitigate risks and
maximize returns by analyzing
market trends, identifying
opportunities, and optimizing
investment portfolios. Through
the use of AI-powered
algorithms, investors can make
data-driven decisions, diversify
their portfolios, and adapt to
changing market conditions. In
this subchapter, we will explore

how AI can revolutionize the way
we approach investment
strategies and unlock new
possibilities for growth and
success.

Overall, this book aims to
provide a comprehensive
overview of how AI can be
harnessed for financial planning
and management. Whether you
are an individual looking to
improve your personal finances
or a business seeking to optimize
your financial operations, the
insights and strategies outlined
in this book will help you
navigate the complexities of
today's financial landscape and
achieve your long-term financial

goals. Let's embark on this exciting journey together and discover the transformative power of AI in financial planning and management.

- Subchapter 1:

Using AI Algorithms for Financial Forecasting

Revolutionizing Financial Forecasting with AI Algorithms In the fast-paced world of finance, staying ahead of the curve is crucial for success. With the rise of artificial intelligence

(AI) technology, financial forecasting has been revolutionized in ways previously unimaginable. In this chapter, we will explore how AI algorithms are transforming the financial industry by providing more accurate and reliable predictions.

Gone are the days of relying solely on human analysts to predict market trends and make investment decisions. AI algorithms have the ability to analyze vast amounts of data in real-time, identifying patterns and trends that human analysts may overlook. This gives financial institutions a competitive edge by allowing them to make informed decisions faster than ever before. One of the key benefits of using AI algorithms for financial forecasting is the ability to minimize risks and maximize profits. By analyzing historical data and market trends, AI algorithms can predict potential market fluctuations and identify opportunities for growth. This allows financial institutions to make strategic decisions that can lead to higher returns on investment.

Another advantage of using AI algorithms for financial forecasting is the ability to automate repetitive tasks. With AI technology, financial institutions can streamline their processes, saving time and resources. This allows analysts to focus on higher-level tasks that require human intervention, such as interpreting complex data and making strategic decisions.

Furthermore, AI algorithms can adapt and learn from new data, continuously improving their accuracy and performance over time. This means that financial institutions can rely on AI technology to provide more accurate and reliable forecasts, giving them a competitive edge in the market.

Overall, the use of AI algorithms for financial forecasting is revolutionizing the industry by providing more accurate predictions, minimizing risks, maximizing profits, automating tasks, and continuously improving performance. As financial institutions continue to embrace AI technology, they will undoubtedly see significant benefits in terms of efficiency, profitability, and competitiveness in the market. In conclusion, AI algorithms are transforming financial forecasting in ways that were previously unimaginable. By harnessing the power of AI technology, financial institutions can stay ahead of the curve and make informed decisions that lead to greater success in the ever-evolving world of finance.

- Subchapter 2:

Automated Budgeting and Expense Tracking with AI

The Rise of AI in Budgeting and Expense Tracking
In the fast-paced world we live in

today, keeping track of our finances can be a daunting task. From budgeting for daily expenses to monitoring our savings and investments, managing money can often feel like a full-time job. But what if there was a way to automate this process and make it easier than ever before? That's where artificial intelligence comes in. AI has revolutionized many aspects of our lives, from driving cars to diagnosing diseases. And now, it's making its mark on personal finance as well. With the help of AI, budgeting and expense tracking have become more efficient, accurate, and user-friendly than ever before. Gone are the days of manually inputting every transaction into a spreadsheet or logging onto multiple accounts to check your balances. AI-powered budgeting and expense tracking tools can now do all of that for you, saving you time and effort in the process.

But how exactly does AI work in this context? The answer lies in its ability to analyze vast amounts of data quickly and accurately. By using machine learning algorithms, AI can identify patterns in your spending habits, predict future expenses, and even offer

personalized recommendations
to help you save money.
One of the key benefits of AI in
budgeting and expense tracking
is its ability to adapt to your
individual needs and preferences.
Whether you prefer to set strict
budgets or simply want to keep
an eye on your spending, AI can
tailor its recommendations to
suit your unique financial goals.
Furthermore, AI can also help
you identify potential areas
where you can cut back on
expenses or optimize your
budget. By analyzing your
spending patterns and trends, AI
can highlight areas where you
may be overspending and

suggest ways to reduce costs without sacrificing your lifestyle. In addition to budgeting, AI can also assist with expense tracking by categorizing your transactions automatically. Whether you're making a purchase at the grocery store or paying a bill online, AI can recognize the type of transaction and assign it to the appropriate category in your budget.

Overall, the rise of AI in budgeting and expense tracking represents a significant step forward in personal finance management. By harnessing the power of machine learning and automation, individuals can now

take control of their finances
with greater ease and precision
than ever before.
In the chapters that follow, we
will delve deeper into the
various ways in which AI is
transforming the world of
personal finance. From
budgeting tips and tricks to
advanced analytics and
forecasting, we will explore the
many ways in which AI can help
you achieve your financial goals.
So sit back, relax, and let AI take
the reins as we embark on this
exciting journey together.

- Subchapter 3:

Minimizing Risks and Maximizing Returns with AI Investment Strategies

Minimizing Risks and Maximizing Returns with AI Investment Strategies
As an experienced copywriter and author of bestselling books, I have spent over a decade studying the intricacies of artificial intelligence (AI) and its impact on various industries. One of the most compelling

applications of AI is in the realm of investment strategies, where its predictive capabilities can help minimize risks and maximize returns for investors. In this chapter, we will explore how AI can be leveraged to create robust investment strategies that outperform traditional methods. By harnessing the power of machine learning algorithms and data analytics, investors can gain valuable insights into market trends and make informed decisions that lead to higher profits.

One of the key benefits of using AI in investment strategies is its ability to process vast amounts of data in real-time. This allows investors to quickly identify emerging opportunities and adjust their portfolios accordingly. By analyzing market trends and historical data, AI algorithms can generate accurate predictions about future price movements, enabling investors to capitalize on profitable trades. Additionally, AI can help investors manage risk more effectively by identifying potential threats to their portfolios. By continuously monitoring market conditions and evaluating the impact of

external factors, such as
economic indicators and
geopolitical events, AI algorithms
can alert investors to potential
risks before they materialize.
This proactive approach to risk
management can help investors
mitigate losses and preserve
capital during market downturns.
Furthermore, AI can assist
investors in diversifying their
portfolios by recommending
investments in a variety of asset
classes. By analyzing correlations
between different financial
instruments and identifying
opportunities for growth, AI
algorithms can help investors
build balanced portfolios that

are resilient to market volatility. This diversification strategy can help spread risk across multiple investments and increase the likelihood of consistent returns over time.

In conclusion, AI offers unprecedented opportunities for investors to minimize risks and maximize returns through sophisticated investment strategies. By leveraging the predictive capabilities of machine learning algorithms and data analytics, investors can gain a competitive edge in the market and achieve superior performance. As AI continues to revolutionize the financial industry, savvy investors who embrace this technology stand to reap substantial rewards in the years to come.

6. Chapter

Building a Strong Online Presence with AI

In today's digital age, having a strong online presence is crucial for businesses and individuals alike. With the rapidly evolving technology landscape, it's important to stay ahead of the curve and leverage cutting-edge tools to stand out in a crowded online space. One such tool that has revolutionized the way we approach online marketing and website optimization is artificial intelligence (AI).

In this chapter, we will explore the ways in which AI can be used to enhance your online presence and drive success in the digital world. We will delve into three key subchapters that highlight the power of AI in different aspects of online marketing and website management.

Subchapter 1: Enhancing SEO Strategies with AI

Search engine optimization (SEO) is a critical component of any successful online marketing strategy. With AI-powered tools, businesses can gain valuable insights into keyword research, competitor analysis, and content optimization. AI algorithms can analyze vast amounts of data to identify trends, predict user behavior, and recommend strategies to improve search engine rankings. By harnessing the power of AI, businesses can stay ahead of the competition and ensure their website ranks high in search engine results pages.

Subchapter 2: Creating Engaging Content with AI Writing Tools

Content is king in the digital world, and creating high-quality, engaging content is essential for attracting and retaining a loyal audience. AI-powered writing tools can help businesses generate compelling content quickly and efficiently. These tools use natural language processing and machine learning algorithms to analyze user preferences, trends, and competitor data to suggest topics, headlines, and writing styles that resonate with target audiences. By leveraging AI writing tools, businesses can streamline their content creation process and deliver relevant, engaging content that drives traffic and conversions.

Subchapter 3: Optimizing Website Performance with AI-driven Insights

Website performance is crucial
for ensuring a positive user
experience and driving
conversions. AI-driven insights
can help businesses identify
areas of improvement on their
websites, such as slow-loading
pages, broken links, and poor
design elements. By analyzing
user behavior, preferences, and
interactions with the website, AI
algorithms can provide
actionable recommendations to
optimize website performance
and improve user engagement.
With AI-driven insights,
businesses can create a seamless
online experience that keeps
users coming back for more.

In this chapter, we will explore the innovative ways in which AI can be used to build a strong online presence and drive success in the digital world. By incorporating AI into your online marketing and website management strategies, you can stay ahead of the competition, attract new customers, and achieve your business goals.

- Subchapter 1:

Enhancing SEO Strategies with AI

The Rise of AI in SEO
In the fast-paced world of digital marketing, staying ahead of the curve is crucial for success. One of the most significant advancements in recent years that has transformed the way we approach search engine optimization (SEO) is artificial intelligence (AI).
AI technologies, such as machine

learning and natural language processing, have revolutionized the way we analyze data, predict trends, and optimize content for search engines. By harnessing the power of AI, marketers can gain valuable insights into user behavior, improve website performance, and ultimately boost their SEO strategies.

In this chapter, we will explore the various ways in which AI is enhancing SEO strategies and providing marketers with a competitive edge in the ever-evolving digital landscape.

The Role of AI in Keyword Research

Keyword research is a

fundamental aspect of any SEO strategy. By identifying the right keywords to target, marketers can ensure that their content is optimized for relevant search queries and reach their target audience effectively. AI has revolutionized the way we conduct keyword research by providing advanced algorithms that can analyze vast amounts of data to identify high-performing keywords.

AI-powered tools, such as Google's Keyword Planner and SEMrush's Keyword Magic Tool, use machine learning algorithms to analyze search trends, competition levels, and user intent to suggest relevant keywords for your content. By leveraging AI in keyword research, marketers can uncover hidden opportunities, discover new keyword variations, and tailor their content to meet the needs of their target audience. Content Optimization with AI Creating high-quality, engaging content is essential for improving organic search rankings and driving traffic to your website. AI has made content optimization more efficient and effective by providing marketers with tools that can analyze content performance, suggest improvements, and even generate content automatically. AI-powered tools, such as Clearscope and MarketMuse, use natural language processing algorithms to analyze content structure, readability, and relevance to target keywords. By leveraging AI in content optimization, marketers can ensure that their content is well-structured, optimized for search engines, and resonates with their target audience.

Predictive Analytics and SEO

Predictive analytics is a powerful tool that allows marketers to anticipate trends, forecast user behavior, and make informed

decisions about their SEO strategies. AI has enabled predictive analytics to become more accurate and reliable by analyzing vast amounts of data to identify patterns, trends, and potential opportunities. AI-powered tools, such as Moz's Keyword Explorer and Ahrefs' Content Gap Tool, use machine learning algorithms to predict search trends, competition levels, and user behavior. By leveraging AI in predictive analytics, marketers can stay ahead of the competition, identify emerging trends, and optimize their SEO strategies for maximum impact.
The Future of AI in SEO

As AI continues to evolve and
become more sophisticated, the
possibilities for its application in
SEO are endless. From voice
search optimization to image
recognition, AI is reshaping the
way we approach search engine
optimization and providing
marketers with new
opportunities to enhance their
strategies.
In the coming years, we can
expect to see AI-powered tools
that can analyze user intent,
personalize content, and
optimize websites for mobile
devices. By embracing AI in SEO,
marketers can stay ahead of the
curve, adapt to changing trends,

and drive meaningful results for their businesses.

Conclusion

AI is revolutionizing the way we approach search engine optimization and providing marketers with new opportunities to enhance their strategies. By leveraging AI in keyword research, content optimization, and predictive analytics, marketers can gain valuable insights, improve website performance, and ultimately boost their SEO efforts.

As the technology continues to evolve, the possibilities for its application in SEO are limitless.

By embracing AI and staying ahead of the curve, marketers can adapt to changing trends, drive meaningful results, and succeed in the competitive world of digital marketing.

- Subchapter 2: Creating Engaging Content with AI Writing Tools

The Rise of AI Writing Tools
In the ever-evolving landscape of content creation, one trend has emerged as a game-changer: the use of artificial intelligence (AI)

writing tools. These sophisticated programs are designed to assist writers in generating engaging, high-quality content in a fraction of the time it would take using traditional methods.

AI writing tools utilize machine learning algorithms to analyze vast amounts of data and produce coherent, relevant text. By leveraging natural language processing (NLP) capabilities, these tools can understand context, tone, and style to create content that mimics human writing. This level of sophistication is unprecedented and has revolutionized the way content is generated across industries.

The adoption of AI writing tools has been swift and widespread, with businesses of all sizes recognizing the value in streamlining their content creation processes. From marketing agencies to e-commerce platforms, organizations are harnessing the power of AI to produce engaging, personalized content at scale.

One of the key benefits of AI writing tools is their ability to improve efficiency and productivity. By automating repetitive tasks such as research, outlining, and drafting, writers can focus their time and energy on higher-level activities, such as strategy development and creative ideation. This not only speeds up the content creation process but also allows for greater creativity and innovation. Furthermore, AI writing tools can help writers overcome common challenges such as writer's block and lack of inspiration. By providing suggestions, prompts, and even generating entire paragraphs or articles, these tools serve as a valuable resource for sparking ideas and maintaining momentum in the writing process.

Another advantage of AI writing

tools is their capacity for optimization and customization. Through the use of data analytics and A/B testing, these tools can analyze the performance of different content variations and recommend improvements to increase engagement and conversion rates. This data-driven approach allows writers to create content that resonates with their target audience and drives desired outcomes. Despite the obvious benefits of AI writing tools, some critics raise concerns about the potential impact on creativity and authenticity. They argue that relying too heavily on AI could result in generic, formulaic content that lacks originality and human touch. However, proponents of AI writing tools counter that these programs are meant to augment, not replace, human creativity, and that when used strategically, they can enhance rather than detract from the quality of content. In conclusion, the rise of AI writing tools represents a significant advancement in content creation, offering writers the opportunity to produce engaging, high-quality content more efficiently and effectively than ever before. By leveraging the power of AI, writers can unlock new possibilities for creativity, productivity, and success in the digital age. As we continue to embrace and harness the potential of AI writing tools, the future of content creation looks brighter than ever.

- Subchapter 3:

Optimizing Website Performance with AI-driven Insights

Introduction to AI-driven
Website Performance
Optimization
In today's digital age, having a
strong online presence is crucial
for businesses to succeed. With
more and more consumers
turning to the internet to
research products and services,
it's essential for companies to
have a website that not only
looks great but also performs
well. Slow loading times,
unresponsive pages, and
outdated content can all
negatively impact a website's
performance and ultimately
drive potential customers away.
This is where artificial
intelligence (AI) comes in. By
harnessing the power of

machine learning algorithms and data analytics, businesses can optimize their website performance to attract and retain customers. In this book, we will explore how AI-driven insights can help businesses improve their website performance and ultimately increase their bottom line.
Understanding Website Performance Metrics
Before diving into how AI can optimize website performance, it's important to understand the key metrics that businesses should be tracking. These metrics can help identify areas for improvement and guide decision-making when it comes to optimizing website

performance.
Some of the key metrics to consider include:
- Page load time: The time it takes for a webpage to fully load. Slow loading times can lead to high bounce rates and decreased user engagement.
- Time to first byte (TTFB): The time it takes for a browser to receive the first byte of data from a server. A high TTFB can indicate server-side issues that need to be addressed.
- Conversion rate: The percentage of website visitors who take a desired action, such as making a purchase or signing up for a newsletter. Improving website performance can help increase conversion rates.

- Bounce rate: The percentage of website visitors who navigate away from the site after viewing only one page. A high bounce rate can indicate a poor user experience.
- Click-through rate (CTR): The percentage of users who click on a specific link or advertisement. Optimizing website performance can help increase CTR and drive traffic to key pages.

By monitoring these metrics and leveraging AI-driven insights, businesses can gain a better understanding of how their website is performing and make data-driven decisions to improve user experience.

Leveraging AI for Website Performance Optimization

AI has the potential to revolutionize website performance optimization by analyzing vast amounts of data and providing actionable insights in real-time. By using machine learning algorithms, businesses can identify patterns, trends, and anomalies that may be impacting website performance. One way AI can help optimize website performance is through predictive analytics. By analyzing historical data and user behavior patterns, AI can predict future website performance metrics and help businesses proactively address potential issues before they impact user experience. Another key benefit of AI-driven insights is personalization. By leveraging AI algorithms, businesses can deliver personalized content and recommendations to users based on their preferences and behavior. This can lead to higher engagement levels and increased conversion rates. Additionally, AI can help businesses improve website performance through A/B testing. By testing different variations of a webpage and analyzing user interactions, businesses can identify which elements are most effective in driving conversions and optimizing user experience.

In this book, we will explore how businesses can leverage AI-driven insights to optimize their website performance and stay ahead of the competition in today's digital landscape.

Case Studies in AI-driven Website Performance Optimization

To illustrate the power of AI in optimizing website performance, let's take a look at some real-world case studies.

Case Study 1: E-commerce Retailer

An e-commerce retailer implemented AI-driven insights to analyze user behavior patterns and identify areas for improvement on their website. By leveraging predictive analytics, they were able to optimize product recommendations, improve load times, and personalize the shopping experience for customers. As a result, the retailer saw a 20% increase in conversion rates and a 15% decrease in bounce rates.

Case Study 2: Software Company

A software company used AI algorithms to analyze user interactions on their website and identify key pain points in the user journey. By implementing A/B testing and personalized content recommendations, they were able to increase user engagement and drive more leads. The company saw a 25% increase in CTR and a 10% increase in overall website performance metrics.

These case studies demonstrate the tangible benefits of

leveraging AI-driven insights for website performance optimization. By harnessing the power of AI, businesses can improve user experience, increase conversions, and stay competitive in today's rapidly evolving digital landscape.
Best Practices for Implementing AI-driven Website Performance Optimization
As businesses look to implement AI-driven insights for website performance optimization, it's important to follow best practices to ensure success.
Some key best practices include:
- Define clear goals and objectives: Before implementing AI algorithms, businesses should define clear goals and objectives

for website performance optimization. Whether the goal is to increase conversions, reduce bounce rates, or improve load times, having a clear strategy in place is essential.

- Collect relevant data: To leverage AI effectively, businesses need to collect relevant data on website performance metrics, user behavior patterns, and user interactions. By gathering comprehensive data sets, businesses can train machine learning algorithms to provide accurate insights.

- Test and iterate: Implementing AI for website performance optimization is an ongoing process that requires testing and iteration. By continuously monitoring performance metrics and refining AI algorithms, businesses can improve user experience and drive better results over time.

By following these best practices and staying abreast of the latest developments in AI technology, businesses can harness the power of AI-driven insights to optimize website performance and achieve their business objectives.

Conclusion

In conclusion, AI has the potential to revolutionize website performance optimization by providing businesses with valuable insights and actionable recommendations. By leveraging machine learning algorithms, predictive analytics, and personalization techniques, businesses can improve user experience, increase conversions, and stay ahead of the competition in today's digital landscape.

In this book, we have explored how AI can help businesses optimize website performance, the key metrics to track, and best practices for implementation. By following these guidelines and staying abreast of the latest AI developments, businesses can unlock the full potential of AI-driven insights and drive success in the digital age.

Remember, the key to success in website performance optimization is to embrace AI as a powerful tool for data-driven decision-making. By harnessing the power of AI, businesses can optimize their website performance and achieve their business objectives in a fast-paced and competitive digital world.

7. Chapter 7:

Streamlining HR Processes with AI

In the modern era, Artificial Intelligence (AI) has revolutionized numerous aspects of business operations, and Human Resources (HR) is no exception. With its ability to analyze vast amounts of data and automate routine tasks, AI has the potential to streamline HR processes, improve efficiency, and enhance employee experiences.

In this book, we will delve into the impact of AI on HR practices, focusing on three key areas: recruitment and candidate screening, employee training and development, and employee retention. Each subchapter will explore how AI technologies can be leveraged to optimize HR functions and drive organizational success.

Subchapter 1 will examine how AI-powered tools and algorithms are transforming the recruitment process, enabling

HR professionals to identify top talent more effectively and efficiently. From automated resume screening to predictive analytics for candidate selection, AI is revolutionizing the way organizations attract and onboard new employees.
In Subchapter 2, we will explore how AI can enhance employee training and development programs, providing personalized learning experiences and actionable insights for skill development. By leveraging AI-powered platforms for training content creation, delivery, and assessment, organizations can upskill their

workforce and drive performance improvements. Finally, Subchapter 3 will focus on how AI-driven insights can help organizations improve employee retention rates. By analyzing employee data and identifying patterns and trends, HR teams can proactively address issues that may impact employee satisfaction and loyalty. From sentiment analysis to predictive modeling, AI offers innovative solutions to boost employee engagement and reduce turnover.

As we embark on this exploration of AI in HR, it is clear that the integration of artificial intelligence technologies holds tremendous potential for transforming traditional HR practices and unlocking new opportunities for organizational growth. Join us on this journey as we uncover the power of AI in streamlining HR processes and shaping the future of work.

- Subchapter 1:

AI-Powered Recruitment and Candidate Screening

The Rise of AI in Recruitment
In the fast-paced world of

recruiting and talent acquisition,
staying ahead of the competition
is crucial. As technology
continues to advance, many
organizations are turning to AI-
powered solutions to streamline
their recruitment processes and
identify top-tier candidates more
efficiently.

One of the most significant
developments in recent years
has been the integration of AI
into recruitment and candidate
screening. With the ability to
analyze vast amounts of data
and identify patterns that
humans may overlook, AI has
revolutionized the way
organizations attract, assess, and

hire talent.

AI-powered recruitment tools leverage machine learning algorithms to sift through resumes, scan social media profiles, and conduct online assessments to identify promising candidates. By automating these tasks, recruiters can spend less time on administrative duties and more time engaging with potential hires.

In addition to enhancing efficiency, AI can also improve the quality of hires by reducing bias in the selection process. Traditional recruitment methods can be influenced by unconscious biases, leading to missed opportunities for qualified candidates. AI, on the other hand, evaluates candidates based on their skills and qualifications, removing subjective factors from the equation.

Furthermore, AI can help organizations scale their recruitment efforts by reaching a larger pool of candidates than ever before. With the ability to analyze thousands of resumes in seconds, AI-powered recruitment tools can quickly identify the most qualified candidates and match them to open positions.

While AI has undoubtedly transformed the recruitment landscape, it is essential to use these tools thoughtfully and ethically. As AI becomes more prevalent in recruitment, organizations must ensure that they are transparent about their use of AI and actively work to mitigate any potential biases in the algorithms.

In the following chapters, we will explore the various ways in which AI is transforming recruitment and candidate screening, from sourcing candidates to conducting interviews and making hiring decisions. By embracing AI-

powered solutions, organizations
can stay competitive in a rapidly
evolving talent market and make
smarter, data-driven decisions
when it comes to hiring.

- Subchapter 2:

Enhancing Employee Training and Development with AI

introduction to AI in Employee
Training and Development

In today's rapidly evolving workplace, the need for continuous skill development and training is more critical than ever. As organizations strive to stay competitive and adapt to the demands of the digital age, they must find innovative ways to enhance their employees' knowledge and capabilities. One such way is through the utilization of artificial intelligence (AI) in employee training and development.

AI has the potential to revolutionize the way we approach learning and development in the workplace. By leveraging AI-powered tools and technologies, organizations can create personalized and adaptive training programs that cater to the unique needs and learning styles of their employees. From virtual reality simulations to chatbots and intelligent tutoring systems, AI offers a wide range of possibilities for enhancing the effectiveness and efficiency of employee training.

In this book, we will explore the various ways in which AI can be used to augment employee training and development. We will delve into the benefits of integrating AI into training programs, the challenges and limitations of AI in this context, and practical examples of AI-driven training solutions that have already proven successful in real-world settings.

The Benefits of AI in Employee Training and Development

There are numerous advantages to incorporating AI into employee training and development initiatives. One of the key benefits is the ability to personalize training programs to better meet the needs of individual learners. AI algorithms can analyze employee data, such as performance metrics and learning preferences, to tailor training content and delivery methods accordingly. This personalized approach not only enhances engagement and motivation but also improves the overall effectiveness of the training program.

Another major benefit of AI in employee training is its capacity for automation. AI-powered tools can automate routine tasks, such as grading assessments and providing feedback, allowing trainers to focus on more strategic aspects of training development. This automation can also help streamline the training process and reduce the time and resources required to deliver training programs.

Furthermore, AI can facilitate continuous learning and development by providing employees with on-demand access to training materials and resources. Through AI-powered platforms, employees can engage in self-paced learning activities, receive instant feedback, and access personalized recommendations for further training opportunities. This accessibility ensures that employees can build and enhance their skills at their own pace, leading to improved performance and job satisfaction. Overall, the benefits of AI in employee training and

development are wide-ranging and significant. From personalized learning experiences to streamlined automation and continuous access to resources, AI has the potential to transform the way organizations approach employee development.
Challenges and Limitations of AI in Employee Training and Development
While the benefits of AI in employee training and development are substantial, there are also challenges and limitations that organizations must consider when implementing AI-driven training

programs. One of the primary challenges is the potential for bias in AI algorithms. If not carefully monitored and controlled, AI systems can inadvertently perpetuate existing biases in training content and evaluation methods, leading to unfair or inaccurate results.

Another challenge is the issue of data privacy and security. AI-powered training programs rely on vast amounts of employee data to function effectively, raising concerns about how this data is collected, stored, and used. Organizations must ensure that appropriate safeguards are in place to protect the privacy and confidentiality of employee information.

Additionally, the use of AI in employee training and development may require significant upfront investment in terms of technology infrastructure and workforce training. Organizations must carefully assess the costs and benefits of implementing AI solutions and be prepared to allocate resources accordingly. Moreover, there is the challenge of ensuring that employees feel comfortable and confident in using AI-powered training tools. Some employees may be

resistant to new technologies or feel overwhelmed by the complexity of AI systems. Organizations must provide adequate training and support to help employees navigate and integrate AI into their learning experiences successfully. Despite these challenges, it is essential for organizations to address them proactively and thoughtfully to maximize the potential of AI in employee training and development.
Chapter 4: Practical Applications of AI in Employee Training and Development
There are numerous ways in which AI can be applied to

enhance employee training and development. One example is the use of virtual reality (VR) simulations to provide immersive and interactive training experiences. VR technology allows employees to practice real-life scenarios in a safe and controlled environment, helping them develop practical skills and improve their decision-making abilities.

Another practical application of AI in training is the use of chatbots to deliver personalized and instant support to employees. Chatbots can answer questions, provide guidance, and offer feedback in real-time, enhancing the learning experience and promoting continuous engagement. Intelligent tutoring systems are another valuable tool for AI-driven training programs. These systems use AI algorithms to adapt training content and difficulty levels based on each employee's performance and progress, ensuring that they receive targeted and effective training.

Furthermore, AI-powered learning management systems (LMS) can help organizations track employee progress, analyze performance data, and generate insights for continuous improvement. By leveraging AI analytics, organizations can identify trends, patterns, and areas for enhancement in their training programs.

Overall, these practical applications of AI in employee training and development demonstrate the diverse and powerful ways in which AI can enhance learning experiences and drive organizational success.

Conclusion

In conclusion, AI has the potential to revolutionize employee training and development by offering personalized, automated, and accessible learning experiences.

While there are challenges and limitations to consider, the benefits of AI in this context are numerous and significant.

By embracing AI-powered training solutions, organizations can create dynamic and effective learning programs that empower employees to develop and grow continuously. With the right strategy, resources, and commitment, organizations can unlock the full potential of AI in employee training and development, driving innovation, productivity, and success in the workplace.

Improving Employee Retention through AI-driven Insights

The Impact of AI on Employee Retention
In today's fast-paced business world, employee retention has become a critical factor in the success of any organization. With the rise of artificial intelligence (AI) technology, companies now have the opportunity to leverage data-

driven insights to improve their employee retention rates. In this chapter, we will explore how AI can be used to analyze employee data, identify patterns and trends, and ultimately create strategies to retain top talent.

The Importance of Employee Retention

Employee retention is a key metric for any organization looking to maintain a competitive edge in the market. High turnover rates can result in increased costs associated with recruiting, hiring, and training new employees, as well as a loss of institutional knowledge and expertise. Additionally, a high

turnover rate can negatively
impact employee morale and
productivity, leading to
decreased overall performance.
In today's job market, employees
have more options than ever
before when it comes to
choosing where they work. With
a growing emphasis on work-life
balance, career development
opportunities, and a positive
company culture, employees are
increasingly looking for
organizations that prioritize their
well-being and growth. As such,
it is essential for companies to
invest in strategies that promote
employee satisfaction and
engagement in order to retain

their top talent.

The Role of AI in Improving Employee Retention

AI technology has revolutionized the way companies collect, analyze, and interpret data. By leveraging AI-driven insights, organizations can gain a deeper understanding of their employees' behaviors, preferences, and performance. This data can be used to identify patterns and trends that may indicate potential turnover risks, allowing companies to proactively address issues before they escalate.

One of the key benefits of using AI for employee retention is its ability to provide real-time insights into employee satisfaction and engagement. By analyzing data from surveys, performance reviews, and other sources, AI algorithms can identify potential red flags such as low job satisfaction, high turnover intentions, or disengagement. This allows companies to take proactive measures to address these issues and improve employee retention rates.

AI can also help companies personalize their retention strategies based on individual employee preferences and needs. By analyzing a wide range of data points, including performance metrics, tenure, demographics, and feedback, AI algorithms can identify patterns and preferences that may indicate which retention strategies are most effective for different groups of employees. This level of personalization can help companies tailor their approaches to meet the unique needs of their workforce, increasing the likelihood of retaining top talent.

Case Study: Leveraging AI to Improve Employee Retention at TechCorp

TechCorp, a leading technology company, was facing challenges with employee retention due to a competitive job market and high demand for skilled tech professionals. In an effort to address this issue, the company implemented an AI-driven retention program aimed at identifying and addressing turnover risks proactively. TechCorp began by collecting and analyzing data from various sources, including employee surveys, performance reviews, and exit interviews. By leveraging AI algorithms, the company was able to identify key factors contributing to turnover, such as low job satisfaction, lack of career development opportunities, and poor work-life balance. Armed with this data, TechCorp was able to develop targeted retention strategies to address these issues and improve employee satisfaction and engagement.

One of the key initiatives implemented by TechCorp was a personalized career development program for employees. By using AI algorithms to analyze individual performance metrics, tenure, and feedback, the company was able to tailor career development plans to meet the unique needs of each employee.

This not only helped to increase employee satisfaction and engagement but also resulted in higher retention rates among top performers.

Another initiative introduced by TechCorp was a flexible work schedule program aimed at promoting work-life balance and reducing burnout. By analyzing data on employee work hours, productivity levels, and stress levels, the company was able to identify opportunities for flexibility in scheduling and remote work options. This led to a significant improvement in employee morale and retention rates, as employees felt more supported and valued by the company.

Overall, TechCorp's AI-driven retention program was a resounding success, resulting in a significant reduction in turnover rates and increased employee satisfaction and engagement. By leveraging data-driven insights and personalized strategies, the company was able to create a workplace environment that prioritized employee well-being and growth, ultimately leading to a more loyal and motivated workforce.

Conclusion

In conclusion, AI technology has the potential to revolutionize the way companies approach employee retention. By leveraging data-driven insights, organizations can gain a deeper understanding of their employees' behaviors, preferences, and performance, allowing them to identify turnover risks proactively and develop targeted retention strategies. Through personalized approaches and proactive measures, companies can create a workplace environment that promotes employee satisfaction, engagement, and loyalty, ultimately leading to improved retention rates and a more resilient workforce. As AI continues to evolve and improve, the possibilities for improving employee retention are endless, making it an essential tool for any organization looking to stay ahead in today's competitive job market.

8. Chapter

Implementing AI for Competitive Advantage

In the rapidly evolving landscape of the business world, companies are constantly seeking ways to gain a competitive edge. One such way is through the implementation of Artificial Intelligence (AI) technologies. AI has the power to revolutionize how businesses operate, offering insights and capabilities that were previously unimaginable. In this book, we will explore how companies can harness the power of AI to not only stay ahead of the competition but to thrive in an increasingly competitive market. Using AI for Competitive Analysis and Benchmarking

In this chapter, we will delve into how AI can be used to analyze market trends, competitors, and customer behavior. By leveraging AI-driven tools and algorithms, companies can gain valuable insights into their industry and make informed decisions based on data rather than intuition. We will also explore how AI can be used for benchmarking purposes, allowing companies to compare their performance against industry standards and identify areas for improvement.

Developing AI-Powered Product Innovation Strategies

Product innovation is crucial for companies looking to differentiate themselves in a crowded market. In this chapter, we will discuss how AI can be used to drive product innovation by analyzing consumer preferences, predicting market trends, and identifying opportunities for new product

development. We will also explore how AI can streamline the product development process, leading to faster time-to-market and increased efficiency.
Staying Ahead of the Competition with AI-driven Marketing
Marketing is another area where AI can provide a significant advantage. In this chapter, we will explore how AI can be used to personalize marketing campaigns, target the right audience, and optimize marketing spend. We will also discuss how AI can be used for predictive analytics, allowing

companies to anticipate market changes and stay one step ahead of the competition.

By the end of this book, readers will have a comprehensive understanding of how AI can be leveraged for competitive advantage in today's fast-paced business environment. Whether you are a seasoned business executive or a budding entrepreneur, this book will provide you with the knowledge and tools needed to succeed in an AI-driven world. So let's dive in and explore the exciting possibilities that AI has to offer for your business.

Using AI for Competitive Analysis and Benchmarking

Introduction to AI in
Competitive Analysis
In today's fast-paced business
environment, staying ahead of
the competition is more
important than ever. With the
rise of artificial intelligence (AI),
companies now have a powerful

tool at their disposal to gain insights into their competitors' strategies and improve their own competitive advantage.

In this chapter, we will explore how AI can be used for competitive analysis and benchmarking, and how it can help companies make smarter decisions and achieve their business goals.

1.1 What is Competitive Analysis?

Competitive analysis is the process of identifying and evaluating your competitors' strengths and weaknesses in order to gain a competitive advantage. By understanding what your competitors are doing and how they are performing, you can make better-informed decisions about your own business strategy.

Traditionally, competitive analysis has been a manual and time-consuming process, involving hours of research and analysis. However, with the advent of AI, this process can now be automated and streamlined, allowing companies to access real-time data and insights on their competitors with minimal effort.

1.2 The Role of AI in Competitive Analysis

AI has the potential to revolutionize competitive

analysis by providing companies with new ways to gather, analyze, and interpret data on their competitors. By using AI algorithms and machine learning techniques, companies can now quickly identify trends, patterns, and opportunities in the market that would have been difficult or impossible to detect using traditional methods.

For example, AI can be used to automatically scrape and analyze data from competitors' websites, social media channels, and other online sources to track their marketing strategies, pricing tactics, and customer feedback. This information can then be used to identify gaps in the market, predict competitors' future moves, and develop more effective strategies to stay ahead.

1.3 Benefits of AI for Competitive Analysis

There are several key benefits of using AI for competitive analysis, including:

- Real-time insights: AI can provide companies with up-to-date information on their competitors' activities, allowing them to react quickly to changes in the market.

- Improved accuracy: AI algorithms can analyze vast amounts of data in a fraction of the time it would take a human

analyst, and with greater accuracy, reducing the risk of errors and bias.
- Enhanced decision-making: By leveraging AI-powered insights, companies can make more informed decisions about their competitive strategy, pricing, product development, and marketing campaigns.
- Competitive advantage: By using AI to gain a deeper understanding of their competitors, companies can identify new opportunities for growth and innovation, and stay ahead in their industry.
Overall, AI has the potential to transform the way companies

approach competitive analysis, enabling them to gain a more comprehensive and actionable understanding of their competitive landscape.

1.4 Challenges and Considerations

While AI offers many benefits for competitive analysis, there are also some challenges and considerations that companies need to be aware of. These include:

- Data privacy and security: Companies need to ensure that they are using AI tools and technologies in a responsible and ethical manner, respecting the privacy of their competitors'

data and complying with
regulations such as GDPR.
- Accuracy and reliability: While
AI algorithms can analyze data at
scale, they are only as good as
the data they are trained on.
Companies need to ensure that
they are using high-quality data
sources and that their AI models
are regularly tested and updated.
- Implementation and
integration: Adopting AI for
competitive analysis requires a
significant investment in
technology, talent, and
infrastructure. Companies need
to carefully plan and execute
their AI initiatives to ensure they
deliver value and align with their

business objectives.

Despite these challenges, the benefits of using AI for competitive analysis far outweigh the risks, and companies that embrace AI as part of their competitive strategy are likely to see significant improvements in their performance and competitiveness.

In the following chapters, we will explore specific AI tools and techniques that companies can use for competitive analysis and benchmarking, and provide practical tips and examples for leveraging AI to gain a competitive edge in their industry.

- Subchapter 2

Developing AI-Powered Product Innovation Strategies

The Rise of AI in Product Innovation
In recent years, artificial intelligence (AI) has been making waves across various industries, revolutionizing the way businesses operate and innovate. From automating mundane tasks

to predicting consumer behavior, AI has the potential to transform the product development process and drive innovation to new heights.

But what exactly is AI, and how can it be harnessed to develop groundbreaking product innovations? In this chapter, we will explore the basics of AI technology and its applications in product development, as well as discuss strategies for leveraging AI to drive innovation in your organization.

The Basics of AI Technology

At its core, AI refers to the simulation of human intelligence processes by machines, particularly computer systems. This includes tasks such as learning, reasoning, problem-solving, perception, and language understanding. AI systems are designed to mimic the cognitive functions of humans, enabling them to perform complex tasks with minimal human intervention. There are several types of AI technologies that are commonly used in product development, including machine learning, natural language processing, computer vision, and robotics. Machine learning, in particular, has gained significant traction in recent years due to its ability to analyze vast amounts of data and derive insights that can inform decision-making and drive innovation.

Natural language processing (NLP) is another key AI technology that enables computers to understand and generate human language. NLP can be used to analyze customer feedback, social media conversations, and market trends, allowing businesses to gain valuable insights into consumer preferences and behavior.

Computer vision is another important AI technology that enables machines to interpret visual information, such as images and videos. This technology can be used to develop innovative products that rely on visual recognition, such as augmented reality (AR) applications and autonomous vehicles.

Finally, robotics is a field of AI that focuses on designing and building machines that can perform physical tasks autonomously. Robotics has the potential to transform industries such as manufacturing, healthcare, and logistics by automating repetitive and dangerous tasks, thereby increasing efficiency and reducing human error.

Applications of AI in Product Development

AI technology has a wide range of applications in product development, from ideation and design to testing and marketing. By harnessing the power of AI, businesses can streamline their product development processes, accelerate time-to-market, and create products that resonate with consumers.

One of the primary applications of AI in product development is predictive analytics, which involves using machine learning algorithms to analyze historical data and predict future trends.

Predictive analytics can help businesses identify market opportunities, anticipate consumer demand, and optimize their product offerings to meet evolving customer needs. Another key application of AI in product development is generative design, which involves using algorithms to automatically generate and evaluate design options based on specified criteria. Generative design can help businesses explore a wider range of design possibilities, optimize product performance, and reduce time and cost in the design process. AI technology can also be used to enhance product testing and quality control processes. For example, machine learning algorithms can analyze product performance data and detect anomalies or defects, enabling businesses to identify and rectify issues before products are released to the market. Furthermore, AI-powered chatbots and virtual assistants can be used to improve customer engagement and support throughout the product development lifecycle. These tools can provide personalized product recommendations, answer customer queries, and gather feedback to inform future product iterations.

Strategies for Leveraging AI in Product Innovation

To truly leverage the power of AI in product innovation, businesses must adopt a strategic approach that aligns AI initiatives with their overarching business goals and objectives. Here are some key strategies for incorporating AI into your product innovation process:

1. Identify Key Areas for AI Implementation: Begin by identifying key areas within your product development process where AI can add value, such as design optimization, market research, or customer

engagement. Prioritize initiatives
that align with your business
objectives and have the
potential to drive significant ROI.
2. Build a Cross-Functional Team:
Develop a cross-functional team
that includes data scientists,
software engineers, product
managers, and domain experts
to collaborate on AI initiatives.
By bringing together diverse
perspectives and expertise, you
can ensure that AI projects are
aligned with business needs and
technical requirements.
3. Invest in Data Infrastructure:
Data is the lifeblood of AI, so it is
essential to invest in robust data
infrastructure that can support

AI initiatives. Ensure that you have access to clean, reliable data sources and implement data governance processes to maintain data quality and integrity.

4. Experiment and Iterate: AI is a rapidly evolving field, so it is important to adopt an experimental mindset and embrace a culture of continuous learning and improvement. Start small with pilot projects and iterate based on feedback and results to refine your AI strategies over time.

5. Measure Success: Define clear metrics and KPIs to measure the success of your AI initiatives and

track progress towards achieving your goals. Regularly monitor and analyze performance data to identify areas for optimization and refinement.

By following these strategies and embracing the power of AI technology, businesses can unlock new opportunities for innovation and drive sustainable growth in an increasingly competitive marketplace. The future of product development belongs to those who are willing to embrace AI and harness its transformative potential.

- Subchapter 3: Staying Ahead of the Competition with AI-driven Market Intelligence

The Rise of Artificial Intelligence in Market Intelligence
In the ever-evolving landscape of business and technology, one tool has emerged as a game-changer for companies looking to stay ahead of the competition: artificial intelligence (AI). With the ability to analyze vast amounts of data at lightning speed, AI has revolutionized the

way companies gather, analyze, and act on market intelligence. But what exactly is AI-driven market intelligence, and how can businesses leverage this powerful tool to stay ahead of the curve in today's fast-paced market? In this chapter, we will explore the rise of AI in market intelligence, its benefits, and how companies can effectively implement AI-driven strategies to gain a competitive edge.

The Evolution of Market Intelligence

Market intelligence has long been a crucial aspect of business strategy, providing companies with valuable insights into market trends, consumer behavior, and competitor activity. Traditionally, market intelligence was gathered through manual research methods such as surveys, focus groups, and industry reports. While effective, these methods were time-consuming and often limited in scope.

Enter AI. With its ability to process and analyze massive amounts of data in real-time, AI has transformed the way companies approach market intelligence. By leveraging machine learning algorithms, AI can quickly identify patterns, trends, and opportunities in vast

datasets that would be impossible for humans to uncover on their own.
The Benefits of AI-driven Market Intelligence
The benefits of AI-driven market intelligence are numerous and far-reaching. One of the key advantages of AI is its ability to provide real-time insights into market conditions, competitor activity, and consumer behavior. By continuously monitoring and analyzing data from various sources, AI can alert businesses to emerging trends and opportunities before they become mainstream. Additionally, AI-driven market

intelligence can help companies make more informed decisions by providing predictive analytics and scenario modeling. By analyzing historical data and identifying patterns, AI can forecast future market trends and help businesses anticipate changes in consumer preferences or competitor strategies.

Furthermore, AI can also streamline the process of gathering and analyzing market intelligence, saving companies time and resources. By automating repetitive tasks such as data collection and analysis, AI allows businesses to focus on strategic decision-making and innovation.

Implementing AI-driven Market Intelligence

While the benefits of AI-driven market intelligence are clear, implementing AI strategies can be challenging for many companies. To effectively leverage AI, businesses must first identify their objectives and define clear goals for their market intelligence efforts. Whether it's monitoring competitor activity, understanding consumer preferences, or predicting market trends, companies must have a clear vision of what they want to achieve with AI.

Next, companies must invest in the right technology and infrastructure to support their AI initiatives. This includes acquiring the necessary tools and software to collect, analyze, and visualize data, as well as training employees on how to use AI effectively. Additionally, companies must ensure that their data is clean, accurate, and up-to-date to ensure the success of their AI-driven market intelligence efforts.

Finally, companies must continuously monitor and evaluate their AI strategies to ensure they are achieving their desired outcomes. By regularly reviewing performance metrics and adjusting strategies as needed, businesses can stay ahead of the competition and capitalize on the power of AI-driven market intelligence.

Staying Ahead of the Competition

In today's fast-paced market, staying ahead of the competition is more important than ever. By leveraging the power of AI-driven market intelligence, companies can gain valuable insights into market trends, competitor activity, and consumer behavior that can help them make informed decisions and drive growth.

As we enter an era where AI is becoming increasingly integrated into business operations, companies that embrace AI-driven market intelligence will have a significant advantage over those that do not. By investing in the right technology, defining clear objectives, and continuously monitoring and evaluating their strategies, companies can position themselves as leaders in their respective industries and stay ahead of the competition for years to come.

In the next chapter, we will explore how companies can use

AI to optimize their marketing strategies and engage with consumers in new and innovative ways. Stay tuned for more insights on how AI is reshaping the business landscape and transforming the way companies operate in today's digital age.

9. Chapter

Scaling Your Business with AI Automation

As we enter the era of artificial intelligence, businesses are faced with the challenge of adapting and evolving to stay competitive in a rapidly changing landscape. In this chapter, we will explore how AI automation can revolutionize the way businesses operate, helping them scale their operations and achieve new levels of efficiency and growth.

Subchapter 1 will focus on streamlining operations and increasing efficiency with AI. We will dive into the various ways in which AI can automate repetitive tasks, optimize processes, and reduce human error. By harnessing the power of AI, businesses can save time and resources, allowing them to focus on strategic initiatives that drive their growth.

In Subchapter 2, we will discuss how AI can help businesses expand their reach and capitalize on growth opportunities. From personalized marketing campaigns to predictive analytics,

AI can provide valuable insights that enable businesses to better understand their customers and target new markets. By leveraging AI, businesses can uncover hidden opportunities for expansion and drive sustainable growth.

Finally, Subchapter 3 will address the scalability challenges that businesses face when implementing AI solutions. From data management to infrastructure requirements, scaling AI initiatives can present unique challenges. However, with the right strategies and tools in place, businesses can effectively manage scalability issues and ensure the successful integration of AI into their operations.

Through these three subchapters, we will explore how AI automation can transform businesses, helping them overcome operational hurdles, unlock growth opportunities, and navigate the complexities of scalability. Join us on this journey as we discover the endless possibilities of scaling your business with AI.

Streamlining Operations and Increasing Efficiency with AI

Understanding Artificial Intelligence

Artificial Intelligence, or AI, is a revolutionary technology that is transforming the way businesses operate. By harnessing the power of machine learning and data analysis, AI can streamline operations, increase efficiency, and drive innovation. In this chapter, we will explore the basics of AI, its applications in business, and how organizations can leverage this technology to achieve their goals.

AI is a branch of computer science that aims to create intelligent machines that can perform tasks typically requiring human intelligence. These tasks include problem-solving, decision-making, natural language processing, and image recognition. AI systems learn from data and experience, enabling them to improve their performance over time.

There are several types of AI, including narrow AI, general AI, and superintelligent AI. Narrow AI is designed to perform specific tasks, such as speech recognition or playing chess. General AI has the ability to perform any intellectual task that a human can do, while superintelligent AI surpasses human intelligence in every way.

In business, AI is being used to automate repetitive tasks, analyze vast amounts of data, and make predictions based on patterns and trends. These capabilities are transforming industries such as finance, healthcare, marketing, and manufacturing. Organizations that embrace AI can gain a competitive edge by improving decision-making, reducing costs, and increasing productivity.

To leverage AI effectively, businesses must understand the different types of AI technologies available, such as machine learning, deep learning, and natural language processing. Machine learning involves training algorithms to learn from data and make predictions, while deep learning uses neural networks to model complex patterns. Natural language processing enables computers to understand and generate human language.

One example of AI in action is

chatbots, which use natural language processing to interact with customers and provide instant support. Chatbots can answer questions, process orders, and handle complaints, saving businesses time and resources. Another example is predictive analytics, which uses AI to forecast future trends and outcomes based on historical data.

Overall, AI has the potential to transform businesses by streamlining operations, increasing efficiency, and driving innovation. By understanding the basics of AI and its applications in business, organizations can harness this technology to achieve their goals and stay ahead of the competition.

In the next chapter, we will explore how AI is being used to streamline operations and increase efficiency in different industries. Stay tuned for real-world examples and practical tips on how to implement AI in your organization.

Expanding Reach and Growth Opportunities with AI

Introduction to Artificial Intelligence

Artificial Intelligence, or AI, has revolutionized the way businesses operate and interact with customers. From personalized marketing campaigns to predictive analytics, AI has opened up a world of possibilities for companies looking to expand their reach and grow their business.

In this chapter, we will explore the basics of AI and how it can be used to drive growth and reach new audiences. We will delve into the different types of AI, including machine learning, natural language processing, and neural networks, and discuss how each can be leveraged to achieve business goals.

But first, let's start by defining what AI actually is. At its core, AI refers to the simulation of human intelligence in machines that are programmed to think and learn like humans. This can include tasks such as problem-solving, speech recognition, and decision-making.

One of the key advantages of AI is its ability to analyze large amounts of data quickly and efficiently. This allows businesses to gain valuable insights into customer behavior, market trends, and competitive landscapes. By harnessing the power of AI, companies can make data-driven decisions that drive growth and increase profits. AI can also be used to automate repetitive tasks, freeing up employees to focus on higher-value activities. This not only increases productivity but also improves job satisfaction among employees. In fact, studies have shown that employees are more engaged and motivated when they are able to focus on tasks that require creativity and critical thinking, rather than mundane tasks.

In the following chapters, we will explore specific use cases of AI in various industries, including retail, healthcare, and finance. We will examine how companies are leveraging AI to improve customer experiences, streamline operations, and drive revenue growth.

So join me on this journey as we explore the endless possibilities of AI and how it can help businesses expand their reach and unlock new growth opportunities. Get ready to embrace the future of artificial intelligence and revolutionize your business in ways you never thought possible.

Managing Scalability Challenges with AI Solutions

Artificial Intelligence (AI) has revolutionized the way businesses operate in today's digital age. From improving efficiency to enhancing customer experience, AI has proven to be a valuable asset for companies looking to stay ahead of the competition. In this guide, we will explore how businesses can leverage AI to expand their reach

and unlock growth opportunities.
Understanding AI
Before we delve into how AI can help businesses expand their reach and grow, it is important to have a basic understanding of what AI is and how it works. AI refers to the simulation of human intelligence processes by machines, particularly computer systems. These processes include learning, reasoning, and self-correction.

AI technologies such as machine learning, natural language processing, and computer vision are all examples of how AI can be applied to various business functions. By analyzing data and

identifying patterns, AI can automate tasks, predict outcomes, and provide insights that can drive decision-making.
Expanding Reach with AI
One of the key ways that businesses can use AI to expand their reach is through personalized marketing. By analyzing customer data and preferences, AI algorithms can tailor marketing messages to individual customers, increasing the likelihood of engagement and conversion.
For example, e-commerce companies can use AI to recommend products to customers based on their

browsing history and purchase behavior. This personalized approach not only enhances the customer experience but also drives sales and loyalty.
AI can also be used to optimize digital advertising campaigns. By analyzing data in real-time, AI algorithms can adjust ad placements, targeting, and messaging to maximize ROI. This level of optimization would be nearly impossible to achieve manually, making AI an invaluable tool for reaching new audiences and driving growth.
Growth Opportunities with AI
In addition to expanding reach, AI can uncover new growth

opportunities for businesses. By analyzing market trends and consumer behavior, AI can identify emerging opportunities and potential threats, allowing businesses to pivot their strategies accordingly.

For example, AI-powered analytics platforms can track competitor activities, customer sentiment, and industry trends, providing businesses with valuable insights that can inform strategic decision-making. By staying ahead of the curve, businesses can capitalize on new opportunities and maintain a competitive edge.

AI can also streamline internal

operations and improve productivity, freeing up resources that can be reinvested into growth initiatives. By automating routine tasks, AI can reduce human error and improve efficiency, allowing employees to focus on higher-value activities that drive innovation and growth.

Conclusion

AI presents endless possibilities for businesses looking to expand their reach and unlock growth opportunities. By leveraging AI technologies such as machine learning, natural language processing, and computer vision, businesses can personalize marketing efforts, optimize advertising campaigns, and uncover new growth opportunities.

To stay ahead of the competition in today's digital age, businesses must embrace AI and harness its power to drive innovation and growth. With the right strategy and implementation, AI can transform businesses and propel them towards success in the ever-evolving marketplace.

10. Chapter

Monetizing AI Technologies for Profit

Welcome to Chapter 10 of our book, where we dive into the fascinating world of monetizing AI technologies for profit. In this chapter, we will explore various strategies and techniques to leverage artificial intelligence for financial gain.

Artificial Intelligence (AI) has become a hot topic in recent years, with businesses across industries racing to implement AI-driven solutions to gain a competitive edge. From chatbots and virtual assistants to predictive analytics and automation, AI technologies are revolutionizing the way companies operate and interact with customers.

In this chapter, we will discuss the different ways you can commercialize AI technologies and services to generate revenue. We will also explore how you can create passive income streams by leveraging AI-driven solutions. Additionally, we will delve into the importance of maximizing return on investment (ROI) through strategic AI investments and partnerships.

Subchapter 1 will focus on the process of commercializing AI technologies and services. We will discuss how you can identify market opportunities, develop AI products and services, and bring them to market successfully. Whether you are a startup looking to launch an AI-powered solution or an established company seeking to expand your AI offerings, this subchapter will provide valuable insights and practical tips.

Subchapter 2 will explore the concept of generating passive

income through AI-driven solutions. We will examine how you can build and monetize AI platforms, develop subscription-based AI services, and create scalable revenue streams. By harnessing the power of AI to automate processes and deliver personalized experiences, you can unlock new sources of passive income and grow your business.

Finally, in Subchapter 3, we will discuss the strategies for maximizing ROI with AI investments and partnerships. We will explore how you can evaluate the potential return on AI projects, mitigate risks, and

drive profitability through
strategic collaborations with AI
vendors and technology partners.
By making informed decisions
and aligning your AI initiatives
with your business goals, you
can achieve long-term success
and financial sustainability.
Join us on this exciting journey
as we explore the endless
possibilities of monetizing AI
technologies for profit. Whether
you are a business leader,
entrepreneur, investor, or AI
enthusiast, this chapter will
equip you with the knowledge
and tools to unlock the full
potential of AI and drive financial
success. Let's dive in and

discover the power of AI in generating profitable returns.

- Subchapter 1: Commercializing AI Technologies and Services

The Rise of Artificial Intelligence In recent years, artificial intelligence (AI) has become one of the most talked-about technologies in the world. From self-driving cars to virtual assistants, AI is transforming industries and shaping the future of our society. But how did we get here? What are the key technologies driving this revolution? And most importantly, how can businesses capitalize on this growing trend? To understand the rise of AI, we must first look back at its origins. The concept of artificial intelligence dates back to the 1950s, when scientists began to explore the idea of creating machines that could think and learn like humans. Over the decades, researchers made significant advancements in the field, developing algorithms and techniques that enabled computers to perform complex tasks and solve problems.

One of the key breakthroughs in AI was the development of machine learning algorithms. These algorithms allow computers to analyze data, identify patterns, and make decisions without being explicitly programmed. This technology has seen widespread adoption in various industries, from finance to healthcare, as companies leverage AI to streamline processes, improve decision-making, and drive innovation. Another major development in AI is the rise of deep learning. Deep learning is a subset of machine learning that uses neural networks to mimic the way the human brain processes information. By training these networks on vast amounts of data, researchers have been able to achieve remarkable results in areas such as image recognition, natural language processing, and speech recognition.

But perhaps the most significant advancement in AI in recent years has been the convergence of AI with other technologies, such as big data, cloud computing, and the Internet of Things (IoT). This convergence has enabled companies to extract valuable insights from massive amounts of data, optimize business operations, and deliver personalized experiences to customers.

As AI continues to evolve, businesses are increasingly looking for ways to commercialize AI technologies and services. One of the key challenges companies face is how to effectively integrate AI into their existing operations and business models. This requires a deep understanding of the capabilities of AI, as well as a strategic approach to implementation.

In addition, companies must also consider the ethical implications of AI. As AI becomes more pervasive in our society, questions around privacy, security, and bias have come to the forefront. It is essential for businesses to prioritize ethical considerations and ensure that AI is used responsibly and transparently.

Overall, the rise of AI presents both opportunities and challenges for businesses. By leveraging the power of AI technologies and services, companies can drive innovation, increase efficiency, and deliver superior customer experiences. However, to succeed in the AI-driven economy, businesses must adapt quickly, invest in talent and resources, and embrace a culture of continuous learning and experimentation.

- Subchapter 2:

Generating Passive Income through AI-driven Solutions

Understanding the Power of AI in Generating Passive Income
In today's digital age, Artificial Intelligence (AI) has become a game-changer in the world of passive income generation. With

its ability to analyze vast amounts of data, make predictions, and automate tasks, AI has opened up new opportunities for individuals and businesses alike to earn money without actively working for it. AI-driven solutions are revolutionizing various industries, from e-commerce to finance, by enabling businesses to streamline operations, personalize customer experiences, and optimize marketing strategies. By harnessing the power of AI, entrepreneurs can leverage data-driven insights to create passive income streams that generate revenue on autopilot. One of the most popular ways to generate passive income through AI is through automated trading systems. These systems use algorithms to analyze market trends, execute trades, and generate profits without human intervention. By leveraging AI's predictive capabilities, investors can maximize their returns and minimize risks in the volatile world of financial markets. Another lucrative opportunity for passive income generation through AI is in the realm of content creation. AI-powered tools like natural language processing and machine learning can generate high-quality articles, videos, and social media posts at scale, allowing content creators to monetize their creations without constantly churning out new material. Furthermore, AI-driven advertising platforms offer passive income opportunities for website owners and bloggers. By using AI algorithms to optimize ad placements, targeting, and performance tracking, publishers can maximize their ad revenue without actively managing campaigns.

In the real estate industry, AI-powered predictive analytics can help investors identify profitable rental properties and predict future market trends. By leveraging AI to analyze property data, investors can make informed decisions that generate passive income through rental yields and property appreciation. Additionally, AI-driven chatbots and virtual assistants are transforming customer service and support functions for businesses. By automating responses to customer inquiries, resolving issues, and providing personalized recommendations, AI-powered bots can enhance customer satisfaction and loyalty, leading to increased sales and revenue.

Overall, the possibilities for generating passive income through AI-driven solutions are endless. By understanding the power of AI and harnessing its capabilities, individuals and businesses can create sustainable revenue streams that grow and scale over time. In the following chapters, we will explore specific AI applications and strategies for building successful passive income businesses in the digital era. Stay tuned for more insights and practical tips on how to leverage AI for financial prosperity.

Maximizing ROI with AI Investments and Partnerships

Understanding the Power of AI in Generating Passive Income
In today's digital age, Artificial Intelligence (AI) has become a game-changer in the world of passive income generation. With its ability to analyze vast amounts of data, make predictions, and automate tasks, AI has opened up new

opportunities for individuals and businesses alike to earn money without actively working for it. AI-driven solutions are revolutionizing various industries, from e-commerce to finance, by enabling businesses to streamline operations, personalize customer experiences, and optimize marketing strategies. By harnessing the power of AI, entrepreneurs can leverage data-driven insights to create passive income streams that generate revenue on autopilot. One of the most popular ways to generate passive income through AI is through automated trading systems. These systems use algorithms to analyze market trends, execute trades, and generate profits without human intervention. By leveraging AI's predictive capabilities, investors can maximize their returns and minimize risks in the volatile world of financial markets. Another lucrative opportunity for passive income generation through AI is in the realm of content creation. AI-powered tools like natural language processing and machine learning can generate high-quality articles, videos, and social media posts at scale, allowing content creators to monetize their

creations without constantly
churning out new material.
Furthermore, AI-driven
advertising platforms offer
passive income opportunities for
website owners and bloggers. By
using AI algorithms to optimize
ad placements, targeting, and
performance tracking, publishers
can maximize their ad revenue
without actively managing
campaigns.

In the real estate industry, AI-
powered predictive analytics can
help investors identify profitable
rental properties and predict
future market trends. By
leveraging AI to analyze property
data, investors can make

informed decisions that generate passive income through rental yields and property appreciation. Additionally, AI-driven chatbots and virtual assistants are transforming customer service and support functions for businesses. By automating responses to customer inquiries, resolving issues, and providing personalized recommendations, AI-powered bots can enhance customer satisfaction and loyalty, leading to increased sales and revenue.

Overall, the possibilities for generating passive income through AI-driven solutions are endless. By understanding the power of AI and harnessing its capabilities, individuals and businesses can create sustainable revenue streams that grow and scale over time. In the following chapters, we will explore specific AI applications and strategies for building successful passive income businesses in the digital era. Stay tuned for more insights and practical tips on how to leverage AI for financial prosperity.

11. Chapter 11

101 Brilliant Prompts

- Guide Writing

- 1. Craft an article on the subject of [INSERT TOPIC]. For instance, compile 21 articles into an e-book and save it as a PDF.

- 2. Propose 5 guide titles regarding [INSERT TOPIC].

- 3. Write an introduction for the guide on [INSERT TOPIC].

- 4. Suggest a cover design for the guide titled [INSERT GUIDE TITLE].

- 5. Create a humorous analogy for [INSERT SUBJECT OF COMPARISON].

- 6. Propose 21 chapters for the book on [INSERT TOPIC].

- 7. Develop a marketing strategy for an e-book on [INSERT TOPIC].

- 8. Correct errors and improve grammar in this text: [INSERT TEXT].

- 9. Enhance punctuation in this text: [INSERT TEXT]

- Marketing Strategy

- 10. Compose a SWOT analysis for your business [DESCRIBE YOUR BUSINESS].

- Analiza SWOT:

- 11. Create an empathy map for your business [DESCRIBE YOUR BUSINESS].:

- 12. Develop an ideal customer avatar for your business [DESCRIBE YOUR BUSINESS].

- 13. Market research. Determine the product or service that would sell best in the [INSERT INDUSTRY] industry.

- **Negotiations**

- 14. Negotiate a lower price for the product [INSERT PRODUCT DESCRIPTION].

- 15. Negotiate installment payments for the product [INSERT PRODUCT DESCRIPTION].

- **Email Responses:**

- •	16. Respond courteously and objectively to the following email [PASTE EMAIL CONTENT].

- •	17. Prepare BATNA for negotiations [DESCRIBE THE NEGOTIATION].

- •	18. List 5 arguments to ease negotiation success regarding [DESCRIBE THE NEGOTIATION TOPIC].

- •	19. The counterpart used these arguments: [INSERT COUNTERPART ARGUMENTS], suggesting a price reduction

during negotiations on [INSERT
NEGOTIATION TOPIC].

*   **Instagram Comments:**

*   20. Write a substantive
comment on the post [PASTE
POST CONTENT].

*   **Job Offers:**

*   21. Create a job offer for
the position of [INSERT

POSITION] in a company specializing in [DESCRIBE THE COMPANY'S BUSINESS].

*   **Research – Information Retrieval and Decision Making:**

*   22. Suggest 5 online tools for [DESCRIBE THE GOAL YOU WANT TO ACHIEVE?].

*   23. Propose 3 free alternatives to the software [INSERT SOFTWARE NAME].

*   **Travel:**

*   24. Suggest 3 European capitals best for a weekend getaway.

*   25. Plan a three-day stay in [INSERT CITY].

*   26. What do you think is worth visiting in [INSERT CITY]? List 5 places.

*   **Excel:**

*   27. Write an Excel formula that [INSERT WHAT THE FORMULA SHOULD DO].

*   **Proofreading:**

- •   28. Check and correct texts for spelling and punctuation. Here is the text: [PASTE TEXT].

- •   **Daily Planning:**

- •   29. Plan my day with [DESCRIBE TASKS TO BE DONE].

- •   30. What activities should I start my day with? [INSERT ALL TASKS FOR TODAY].

- •   30. Od jakich czynności powinienem zacząć dzień [WPISZ WSZYSTKIE ZADANIA NA

- •   31. Here is my task list for today. Prioritize the tasks. My tasks for today are [LIST TASKS].

- 	32. Break down my big goal [INSERT GOAL] into a list of 10 smaller tasks.

- 	33. How can I achieve the big goal [INSERT GOAL] through small steps? List those small steps.

- 	**Decision Making:**

- 	34. I can't decide between [INSERT OPTION A] and [INSERT OPTION B]. How do you think I can make the best choice?

- 	**Stimulating Creativity:**

- •   35. Suggest 5 names for my product. The product is used for [DESCRIBE THE PRODUCT]

- •   **Brand Visualization and Color Scheme:**

- •   **Brand Identity:**

- •   36. Propose 3 brand colors for the [INSERT INDUSTRY] industry. Provide color codes.

- •   34. Propose the appearance and name of a

corporate mascot for the [INSERT INDUSTRY] industry.

- 35. Design and describe a logo idea for a company in the [INSERT INDUSTRY] industry. The company specializes in [INSERT COMPANY'S BUSINESS].

- **Business Strategy:**

- 36. List 5 elements on which a company in the [INSERT INDUSTRY] industry can build its competitive advantage.

- 37. Conduct a SWOT analysis for a company in the [INSERT INDUSTRY] industry. Describe the weaknesses and strengths. [INSERT COMPANY'S WEAKNESSES AND STRENGTHS]

* 38. Establish a pricing strategy for the [INSERT PRODUCT OR SERVICE].

* 39. What can a Magent Lead be in the case of a company in the [INSERT INDUSTRY] industry?

* *Lead Magenta:*

* 40. Describe the ideal customer avatar in the [INSERT INDUSTRY] industry.

* 41. Write a 3-minute speech introducing your company [INSERT COMPANY DESCRIPTION].

- 42. Describe what the future holds for the [INSERT INDUSTRY] industry.

- 43. Write an Instagram post about [INSERT TOPIC].

- 44. Craft an Instagram post listing 5 reasons to buy [INSERT PRODUCT].

- 45. Write a post on Instagram that builds an email list for the [INSERT INDUSTRY] industry.

- 46. Compose a Facebook post outlining 7 benefits of buying [INSERT PRODUCT].

*   47. Write 10 ideas for Facebook posts for the [INSERT INDUSTRY] industry.

*   48. Compose a LinkedIn post promoting [INSERT PRODUCT/SERVICE].

*   49. Create an Instagram post with tips on [INSERT TOPIC].

*   50. Develop a Facebook post announcing an upcoming industry event [INSERT INDUSTRY].

*   51. Write an Instagram post showcasing a customer using [INSERT PRODUCT].

- • 52. Compose a Twitter post encouraging visits to our website in the [INSERT INDUSTRY] industry.

- • 53. Write a LinkedIn post about the latest industry trends in [INSERT INDUSTRY].

- • 54. Create an Instagram post showing the "behind the scenes" life of [INSERT COMPANY'S BUSINESS].

- • 55. Write a Facebook post informing about a new blog post related to [

- • 56. Craft a LinkedIn post celebrating recent achievements. Our success is [INSERT SUCCESS].

- 57. Compose an Instagram post promoting a contest with prizes for [INSERT PRODUCT].

- 58. Write a Twitter post presenting the latest report on [INSERT TOPIC].

- 59. Compose a LinkedIn post featuring the Employee of the Month. Here's a brief description of the employee [INSERT EMPLOYEE DESCRIPTION].

- 60. Write a Facebook post showcasing special offers for [INSERT PRODUCT].

- 61. Craft an Instagram post with an interesting fact about the [INSERT INDUSTRY].

- 62. Compose a Twitter post with quotes from satisfied customers in the [INSERT INDUSTRY].

- 63. Write a LinkedIn post discussing how our products help customers. Here's a brief description of the products [INSERT BRIEF PRODUCT DESCRIPTION].

- 64. Compose a Facebook post sharing our company values.

- •   65. Craft an Instagram post highlighting our commitment to sustainable development.

- •   66. Write a Twitter post with tips for newcomers in the [INSERT INDUSTRY].

- •   67. Compose a LinkedIn post discussing current industry trends in [INSERT INDUSTRY].

- •   68. Craft an Instagram post announcing a new partnership. The partner is [INSERT PARTNER DESCRIPTION].

- •   69. Write a Twitter post showcasing the production process creatively using [INSERT PRODUCT].

- •   70. Compose a LinkedIn post sharing a press article about the company. The article is about [INSERT ARTICLE DESCRIPTION].

- •   71. Write a Facebook post promoting the latest job opening at the company. Here's the job description [INSERT JOB DESCRIPTION].

- •   **Increasing Comments on Social Media:**

- •   72. Write an Instagram post to increase comments. The profile is about [INSERT PROFILE TOPIC].

- 73. Craft an Instagram post to spark discussions and generate many comments in the [INSERT INDUSTRY] industry.

- 74. Create a Facebook post that encourages interaction and comments by asking opinions about [INSERT TOPIC].

- 75. Write an Instagram post that inspires users to share their experiences related to [INSERT TOPIC].

- 76. Create a Twitter post encouraging discussion by asking an open-ended question about [INSERT

- 77. Write a LinkedIn post to increase comments by asking for tips and advice on [INSERT TOPIC].

- 78. Craft an Instagram post that includes a contest for the most creative comment about [INSERT TOPIC].

- 79. Write a Facebook post that increases engagement by creating a survey about [INSERT TOPIC].

- 80. Craft a Twitter post that increases comments by asking for the most important lessons

people have learned in the
[INSERT INDUSTRY] industry.

•	81. Write a LinkedIn post
that sparks a discussion about
the future of the [INSERT
INDUSTRY] industry.

•	82. Create an Instagram
post that increases comments by
asking for opinions on the latest
trend in the [INSERT INDUSTRY]
industry.

•	83. Write a Facebook post
that increases comments by
asking for opinions on our
favorite thing about [INSERT
TOPIC].

- 84. Craft a Twitter post that increases comments by asking for predictions on the future of the [INSERT INDUSTRY] industry.

- 85. Write a LinkedIn post that increases comments by asking for opinions on our latest product [INSERT PRODUCT].

- 86. Create an Instagram post that increases comments by asking for the most significant challenges people have faced in the [INSERT INDUSTRY] industry.

- 87. Write a Facebook post that increases comments by asking for successes people

- 88. Write a Facebook post that captures audience interest in [INSERT PRODUCT].

- 89. Craft an Instagram post that piques curiosity in [INSERT PROFILE TOPICS].

- 90. Write a Facebook post with 7 fascinating facts about the [INSERT INDUSTRY] industry.

- 91. Compose a LinkedIn post to generate interest by presenting an unusual use of [INSERT PRODUCT].

- 92. Write a Twitter post to capture interest by telling the founder's story of [INSERT COMPANY NAME].

- 93. Compose an Instagram post that presents inspiring stories of customers using [INSERT PRODUCT].

- 94. Write a Facebook post that shares the latest trends in the [INSERT INDUSTRY] industry.

- 95. Craft a LinkedIn post to generate interest by comparing our product [INSERT PRODUCT] with a competitor's product.

- 96. Write a Twitter post to capture interest by showing the "behind the scenes" production process of [INSERT PRODUCT].

- 97. Compose an Instagram post presenting creative ways to use [INSERT PRODUCT].

- 98. Write a Facebook post that captures curiosity by debunking common myths and revealing the truth about [INSERT INDUSTRY].

- 99. Compose a LinkedIn post that engages by showing the impact of our product [INSERT PRODUCT] on the local community.

- 100. Write a Twitter post that captures interest by sharing statistics about the company's achievements in the [INSERT INDUSTRY] industry.

- 101. Compose an Instagram post that captivates interest by presenting unexpected benefits of using [INSERT PRODUCT].

I wish you good luck !

Table of contents